Crisis Control

IN THE NEW MILLENNIUM

Seven Key Principles for Your Financial Prosperity

Larry Burkett

A
JANET
THOMA
BOOK

THOMAS NELSON PUBLISHERS
Nashville

Published in Nashville, Tennessee, by Thomas Nelson, Inc.

Scripture quotations are from the NEW AMERICAN STANDARD BIBLE®, © Copyright The Lockman Foundation 1960, 1962, 1963, 1968, 1971, 1972, 1973, 1975, 1977, 1995. Used by permission.

Edited by Adeline Griffith, Christian Financial Concepts.

Library of Congress Cataloging-in-Publication Data

Burkett, Larry.
   Crisis control in the new millennium : seven key principles for your finan-
cial prosperity / Larry Burkett.
      p.   cm.
   Includes bibliographical references.
   ISBN 0-7852-6939-8
   1. Investments. 2. Year 2000 date conversion (Computer systems) I. Title.
HG4521.B788   1999
332.6—dc21   99-43088
                                                                                    CIP

Printed in the United States of America
1 2 3 4 5 6 BVG 04 03 02 01 00 99

CONTENTS

Contents

ACKNOWLEDGMENTS

I would like to gratefully acknowledge some of the people who made this book possible. Without their help, I could not have written it.

Marcia Moore, my assistant, who typed and reviewed this manuscript.

Jodi Berndt, who took my taped messages and converted them to paper.

Adeline Griffith, my editor, who screened every word, jot, and tittle.

Jerry Tuma, Jerry Webb, Ken Franke, and Jim Shoemaker, who contributed their considerable expertise to provide me with good technical data.

To all: Thank You!

—Larry

INTRODUCTION

If you are reading this book, I suspect you are a loyal reader who understands that I am not some kind of a wild-eyed fanatic. Yet, as I began writing this book about the year 2000 and beyond, the question I had to ask myself was, Why bother? A lot of people won't understand the why behind this type of book. Why not just stick to noncontroversial topics like tithing or how to buy a home? Or, should Christians buy new cars, used cars, or lease rather than purchase?

After all, these would be easier topics to cover, and the answers would not generate a lot of controversy from a biblical perspective. The reason I have written this book is that, in truth, I still see a large, looming economic problem on which virtually no one else is reporting.

Am I the only person who recognizes this problem? I think not. Chairman of the Federal Reserve Board Dr. Alan Greenspan also sees the crisis on our horizon and has spoken out about it several times, as have other leading economists. However, the majority of economists and financial planners, Christian or otherwise, have announced that our economy can continue to expand indefinitely and that there are no serious, potential problems.

Introduction

Not long ago, a Christian financial planner, who is not very successful in his own right, wrote a book in which he attacked my previous book, *The Coming Economic Earthquake* (Moody Press, 1991). His comment was that if you had followed the advice of "a well-known Christian economist," you would have missed the largest bull market in the history of the stock market. (I believe that is not true, by the way.) But in *The Coming Economic Earthquake,* I did *not* say that I thought the economy was going to take a nosedive in 1991—or even in 1999. I said that if we did not change our ways we would experience a huge economic crisis sometime after the turn of the century.

Fortunately, with the election of a new Congress in 1994, we did—at least in the short term—change our ways. But we still have not dealt with the underlying problems of the way we handle our private and public monies. All we've done is generate enough money to cover them.

For example, as I write, two potential problems are looming over our heads. First, there is the inflated value of our stock market. We are developing what traditionally has been called a "bubble." We'll consider the *bubble economy* fully later, so let's look at our second potential problem, which I call the *cruising economy.*

Our country's money-handlers continue to "cruise" as if we face no financial threats, even when nations around the rest of the world have slowed down (in either a major *recession* or a *depression*—the difference being how long their economy has been stagnant). At this point, it appears the travails that have overtaken the rest of the world have left us virtually unaffected. But I do not believe this is possible in the long term.

Ask yourself: "Is it possible for the United States to lose *30 to 50 percent of its export market* and not experience some economic impact?" It is true that we haven't seen this loss reflected in obvious ways—at least not yet. America's economy still seems to be sailing along, while other countries seem to be either "stuck" in the doldrums or smashed on the rocks. Whenever our economy turns down—and I believe it is *when,* not *if*—American workers are going to bear a heavy burden for all the cheap imports fueling our bargain-basement economy.

Look at our perilous personal financial practices. The level of consumer debt in America continues to escalate, while the savings rate continues to decline. Many consumers are "upside-down" in loans—and not just on automobiles, on which they owe more than the vehicles are worth. They also are upside-down in loans on their houses—through "creative financing."

Mortgage companies advertise their willingness to lend owners 125 percent of the equity value in their homes. What will happen when many of these home owners experience a financial crunch? Are they going to maintain their homes and continue paying back more money than their homes are worth? Will they continue monthly payments on credit card debts that often exceed their net worth, or will they just give the homes back and walk away from a bad deal, leaving banks and credit issuers to absorb the loss? Look at the ethics of our society. What do you think?

An Overview of Y2K

Whenever I mention finances and the year 2000, people always ask me about the Y2K bug. Some Christians think it will cause no inconvenience at all; others believe it will usher in the apocalypse. As I am writing this book in mid-1999, we are facing all of the potential challenges of Y2K compliance. I have listened to both sides of the Y2K debate and reviewed all the available data. Along with my staff at Christian Financial Concepts, I have been looking at this issue diligently for nearly two years, and after a thorough analysis of all available literature on Y2K, including House of Representatives and Senate testimonial data, I have come to two basic conclusions.

First, in the United States, the majority of our basic utilities (transportation, power, light, and water) will remain in operation with localized, sporadic interruptions, although this will not necessarily be true in substantial portions of the rest of the world. Second, the world's economy (in which the U.S. is a major participant) has the potential of suffering a huge economic hit as a direct result of Y2K. In future chapters we will look at Y2K issues, so for now I just want to acknowledge that I believe it will present a challenge to our seemingly invincible economy.

Stock Speculation

It is a fact that many of my close friends in business and economics agree there is a significant problem looming in this economy: the inflated value of the stock market. But most of them are hesitant about speaking up. Why? Many of them earn their livings in the financial services industry, and if they speak out they will lose clients who believe we'll have continued unlimited growth. If they adopt a more conservative investment philosophy, their clients will go elsewhere; and so they bide their time and hold their tongues.

Many financial advisors are more conservative in their personal finances than they are with their clients' money. They believe personally that the economy is on shaky ground, that it has run its limit, and that we are likely to experience a downturn in the near future. But clients don't pay financial advisors management fees to park their funds in money market accounts or certificates of deposit (CDs). Advisors attract clients by participating in the high returns being made in the stock market. This is what most clients expect. I have talked with many professionals in the writing of this book, and virtually all of them agree on one thing: *this economy defies logic.*

The situation reminds me of W. Somerset Maugham's comment: "There are three rules for writing a novel. Unfortunately, no one knows what they are." In the same way, there are hard-and-fast rules in economics; but no one seems to agree on what they are right now. Many of today's hottest investors have never experienced a bear market. Because of their inexperience, they accept the logic that the rules of economics have changed. Unfortunately, they believe they are somehow *driving* the current bull market, rather than *riding* its wave. They don't fully understand that historical norms aren't artificial restrictions; they are the normal way markets and economies tend to function.

Right now the norms are skewed, and skewed norms tend to correct themselves. For instance, when historically the leading markets' stocks have sold for 11 to 14 times their annual earnings per share and now they're selling for 10 times that (or more).

Historically, we know that when the economy does defy logic it tends to right itself; when it is oversold, it tends to retreat; when it is undersold, it tends to advance. Like the old cliché I heard in economics school, "Everything that goes around comes around!" In other words, if it's up, then it will go down; if it's down, it will come back up. We are well overdue for a correction in this "up" economy. Nobody knows the future—not me and not anyone else. But we do know the past; we know that George Santayana was correct when he said, "Those who fail to learn from the past are doomed to repeat it."

I could be wrong about the timing; I have been in the past and probably will be again, but the fundamental rules haven't changed. All I can do is look at the current facts, weigh them against the historical facts, and try to come to a logical conclusion. Some of my objectivity is muted by the belief that God is going to judge our nation and our society for our wickedness. This run-up in the economy looks like a great opportunity to do just that; however, that really is just my opinion!

Make Your Choices

If, after having read this entire book, you come to another conclusion and decide that the economy is going to grow unchecked for another 10 years—or forever—I'd really like to know how and why. Even if my analysis is off, if you follow my advice, the worst that can happen is that you'll miss some potential profits by being out of the market (in part) for a few months. On the other hand, if my analysis is correct, you'll miss a lot of grief and a substantial loss. Whether you believe that our economy will continue growing like crazy or you think the "honeymoon" may end soon, you will be faced with some Y2K-related decisions throughout the year 2000. (Only 12 to 14 percent of Y2K problems are expected to occur in January 2000.)[1]

There are a lot of positives in this economy right now. Huge amounts of money are pouring into the stock market—including a lot of foreign money—and millions of Americans are doing their primary investing through company retirement plans: 401(k)s, 403(b)s, IRAs, and even IRA/SEPs. Therefore, there's a lot of money to keep feeding the market. If all that is necessary for the market to grow is to have more money flow in, then logically we should expect this market to continue growing. But money is only one factor. There have been many past economic booms similar to this one, when massive amounts of money were flowing into the market—until someone decided that it had gone too far. This has happened, and it will happen again. Then the economy will reverse itself very quickly.

How will you know whether my evaluation of Y2K is right or wrong? You really won't know until it's too late for a second choice. You'll have to commit to one course or the other *before* the outcome is known.

But to help you make your decision, let me use an example by William James, an early pioneer in psychology. He called it "Life's Living Option." Suppose you're in a vehicle stalled on a railroad track, and a powerful locomotive is headed toward you. According to William James, you would need to know these four facts.

1. You have a choice to make: You can stay in the car and try to get it started or get out of your vehicle and seek personal safety.

2. You have the ability to make that choice.
3. There is a consequence to your choice: life if you get out, possible death if you stay in.
4. But while you are choosing, you are *in* one of the choices; you are in the vehicle. The longer you stay, trying to start your car, the more limited your options become.[2]

Do you understand the connection I am trying to make to your financial decisions?

1. My personal evaluations about our economy present you with choices.
2. You have the ability to weigh the information and choose for yourself.
3. Your choices will create outcomes.
4. But while you are deciding, you are already *in* a decision. If you wait too long and others decide to sell off their holdings and sit out Y2K, your options will be limited.

Ultimately, you must read, you must analyze, and you must make your own decisions. Mine is only one source for information; and there are probably other sources that you should read as well. Am I claiming that this book is prophetic? Not at all. I am not a prophet of the Lord (as I've said in every book I've written on economics). I simply try to look at where we are, compare that to historical norms, and then try to determine where we're going.

The first half of this book looks at our economy, the stock market, and the impact of the new millennium. The second half of this book covers some timeless principles that create prosperity, irrespective of what's going on in the economy. The basis for all wealth is God's Word, which tells us that wise planning is what we should be doing. (See Proverbs 16:3, 9, 19:21.)

So, what do I want you to do as a result of reading this book? I am praying that you and your spouse will keep an open mind as you read this book. Women tend to be the readers in America, so if you are a woman, I encourage you to highlight the passages you would like your spouse to read. If you agree with the points I've made and my logic outweighs the logic of others you have read and listened to, you will need to do something! By the time this book is published, you will have very little time to respond—you will be "knee-deep" in Life's Living Option! But, before making any financial decision, pray about it.

If what I'm saying strikes a chord with you, the message is going to come through loud and clear. If it doesn't, just disregard it and sell this book at your next garage sale for a quarter or so.

Nothing in economics is guaranteed or certain. The economy and the stock market reflect the attitudes and values of the people investing their money. When Franklin Delano Roosevelt said, "The only thing we have to fear is fear itself," he was talking about the Great Depression and the financial panic that exacerbated it. In economic history, we see that when a preponderance of people are confident, the economy grows and the stock market expands. When the majority of people are panicked or fearful, the economy and the stock market contract. It really is that simple.

Historical Comparisons

In writing this book, I gathered headlines from 1927 to 1935 and found many astounding articles leading up to 1929 that stimulated my thinking. If I simply substituted 1999 for the date on some of these articles, many of them could have been written this year.

Perhaps the similarities are totally coincidental, or perhaps my thoughts have been molded more by studying the Great Depression than anything else; but the parallels are remarkable. On one side are a few world-renowned economists who are warning of an impending market setback. On the other side is an entire cadre of industry and academic economists who believe the stock market is still a great value, that the economy is fundamentally sound, and that technology will overcome all economic ills. The same parallel occurred in 1929!

It is not my overactive imagination. In his article in *Fortune* magazine, Herb Greenberg has written the following.

> If you've been feeling queasy about the stock market and want to feel queasier still, dig up a copy of *Security Analysis,* the 1934 classic by Benjamin Graham and David Dodd. Among other things, it's one of billionaire Warren Buffett's favorite investment books. Their post mortem of the 1929 stock market crash could easily have been written about the 1990s . . . They preached old-fashioned analysis and warned about losing sight of a stock's value in volatile markets when the attention is bound to be diverted from the investment question to the speculative question, whether the market is near its low or high point. This difficulty was so overshadowing in the years between 1927 and 33 that common stock investment virtually ceased to have any sound practical significance during that period of time.[3]

Although I have been involved in personal finances and helping families for the last 26 years, I realize that I can be misled, just like anybody else. So, even though the *parallels* leading up to the '29 calamity are strikingly similar, they may be only that: statistical coincidences. However, maybe not.

I am not a pessimist by nature; in fact, I believe there will continue to be many opportunities for making money in any economy (whether it is a bull market or a bear market) *if you position yourself properly.* I only wish more Christian families would use the up cycles to get out of debt, rather than to get further into debt. I personally find it difficult to see how we can sustain this growth cycle in the face of ever-increasing government and consumer debt, not to mention the Y2K event.

Contrary to popular opinion, our government does not have less debt. It has more! Through tricky accounting, where funds are borrowed from trust accounts and made to look like assets, much of the debt is hidden from the public, but a day of reckoning is coming. One day those who are paying into the system will want to draw from the system.

On the other side, a book called *The Dow One Million* advances a compelling argument that technologies being developed today will ultimately drive the stock market over the *one-million-point* mark. An argument is made that the technologies now driving our economy are equivalent to the technologies that drove the railroads in the 19th century and brought us the radio, television, and computer technologies that built our current economy. It is a good argument, and I personally believe that *the 21st century will host the largest technology boom ever seen in history.* But will it be built on uninterrupted growth? That's the question addressed in this book.

Having considered all the evidence, I am still convinced that we will hit a major bump in this road to prosperity. I don't doubt that we will recover again, the economy will resume its growth, and advancing technology will drive our economy through the early decades of the 21st century. According to our history, we can expect that huge profits will be made by some, but large potential losses await the naive, who believe technology is the answer to all economic ills.

Very possibly, this is the last book I will write on finances. I feel I have shared everything about money that I know. The information I offer in the first part of this book is my evaluation of what may happen in the near term.

The information offered in the second part of this book is God's Word on finances, and it's timeless. These biblical principles, based upon the Word of God, are irrefutable and immutable. They will work irrespective of the economy.

If God decided to chasten America for our disobedience, the best-laid plans won't resolve the crisis that would ensue. No one knows when God's patience will run out. The best way to prepare for that eventuality is to live by His plan now. Then you won't be like the foolish virgins described in Matthew 25—scurrying around, trying to get ready.

Right or wrong, for better or for worse, I have written what I believe to be the best analysis of the facts at hand.

---

1. *www.gartner.com/y2k.*
2. My first understanding of James' concept was through a gospel tract written by psychologist Dr. Henry Brandt, who used these two scenarios to explain that until we make a decision to trust Jesus Christ as our Savior, we are in Life's *Greatest* Living Option. We have a choice to make: to receive Him and His gift of eternal life or to continue life without Him. God has given us the ability to choose. There is a consequence to our choice: eternal life in heaven with Him if we receive Him, or eternal separation from Him in hell if we reject Him. But while we are choosing, we are in one of the choices already: we are headed toward eternity without Him.
3. "Is it 1997 or 1929? Ominous Echoes from the Great Crash," *Fortune,* October 13, 1997.

PART I

AN ECONOMIC LOOK AT
2000 AND BEYOND

What Happened
to the Earthquake?

I wrote a book in late 1991, *The Coming Economic Earthquake*, the gist of which was that the U.S. government was spending too much money (significantly more, in fact, than it generated each year in tax revenues) and that if this decades-old trend were not reversed, we were headed for an economic collapse of historic proportions. As with all books dealing with future events, I approached the writing of *Earthquake* with some fear and trepidation. But I felt that our national debt and annual deficit were out of control and would eventually (perhaps at the turn of the century) bring our economy to its knees. The book did more than just attack the national debt; it also shed some light on our growing Social Security and Medicare problems and the rising tide of consumer debt.

The book became a national best-seller, and in 1993 Congressman Frank Wolf (R-Virginia) stood on the floor of the House of Representatives and read aloud sections of the book to the members of Congress. In 1994 I revised and updated the book to include several chapters dealing with the Clinton agenda. Combined sales of the 1991 and 1994 versions of *The*

Coming Economic Earthquake exceeded 800,000 copies. To some degree this book influenced the 1994 elections, because several Republican leaders adopted its theme.

That's the good news. The bad news is that in the years following the book's publication I received several letters from readers who pulled their money out of the stock market and otherwise "hunkered down" in anticipation of the economic earthquake. They all wanted to know, especially those who missed the stock market surge, "Why didn't the earthquake you predicted happen?" Interestingly, I continue to receive criticism from Christians in the financial planning field who are trying to say they knew we would not have an economic downturn. To them I would say, "The verdict is not in yet." I said in the book, and still believe, that whatever financial crisis we face would occur around the turn of the century, plus or minus.

Two points need to be made. First, nobody knows the future—not me and not anyone else. All anyone can do is look at the facts and try to draw some conclusions. Second, I never recommended that people cash out of the market—unless they felt God was directing them to pay off their homes.

However, I do recommend that Christians get out of debt, including their homes. God's best is to be totally debt free. Clearly, the majority of families today are carrying too much debt! You can't be financially bound and spiritually free. If that means cashing out, so be it!

The question "Where *is* the earthquake?" is legitimate. Many of my faithful readers have surely asked that question, as I have. It is for them and for the ones who are trying to make sense out of our financially uncertain times that I am writing this chapter and, ultimately, this book. As I write this, inflation in America is virtually nonexistent, unemployment numbers are the lowest they have been in years, and the stock market continues to hit new highs almost daily. And, according to *Wall Street Journal* columnists James K. Glassman and Kevin A. Hassett, this is only the beginning. The Dow, they say, could comfortably and reasonably hit 36,000—and sooner, rather than later.[1]

In other words, we have entered an era of unlimited economic prosperity—when deficits, debts, and interest payments no longer matter; stock prices are no longer tied to company earnings; working is stupid; and "day trading" is smart. Finally we have discovered Utopia. We no longer need to raise and sell pigs; Americans are content to buy and sell "squeal." Now *that's* something that would register on the economic Richter scale!

Bear in mind that in all economies, good and bad, there will be voices of gloom and of glee. Therefore, somebody *has* to be right. Federal Reserve Chairman Alan Greenspan has issued warnings for two years that the market and the economy are overheated and poised for a downturn. Since Dr. Greenspan first issued that ominous warning, if you had also heeded his advice you would have missed a 55 percent rise in the market. Does that mean Dr. Greenspan is wrong? Only today!

Observant readers of *The Coming Economic Earthquake* will recall that economies tend to run in cycles. This graph, which charts the progress of our economy from 1812 to 1990, illustrates the historical pattern of market highs and lows.

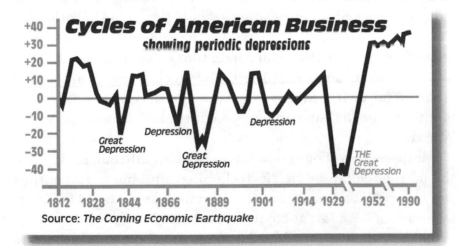

Cycles of American Business
showing periodic depressions

Source: *The Coming Economic Earthquake*

3

One real concern when I wrote *The Coming Economic Earthquake* in 1991 was that we could realistically anticipate an economic downturn to occur about 70 years after the Great Depression, or, in other words, *around the turn of the century.* I never said that I thought our economy would tumble in 1993, '94, or '95; rather, my sights were set much closer to the year 2000. And, despite rosy forecasts from analysts like Glassman and Hassett, I still believe we are in for a major economic and market "adjustment" in the near future—that is, unless we really have found a way to overrule all the fundamental rules of economics. Timing is impossible to predict, but the basic rules of (biblical) economics will always prove to be correct—given enough time.

Can I be sure that 2000 will be *the* year? Of course not! As John Kenneth Galbraith once said, "Only a fool tries to predict the future."[2] But you don't have to look very far to see trouble brewing and, in many cases, boiling over. The truly amazing part is that the U.S. economy has escaped the chaos thus far. If I had written *The Coming Economic Earthquake* in Russia, Indonesia, or Japan, it would still be a best-seller in those countries.

The virtual collapse of economies around the world rivals that of the Great Depression. In fact, if the U.S. economy had followed suit (or if it should), the headlines would have read, "Worldwide Depression Threatens Industrialized Society." But as any student of economic history will agree, the Great Depression didn't just happen in October of 1929. The stock market rallied and slumped for nearly three years following the crash, finally bottoming out in 1933 and dragging on until the U.S. entered World War II.

Many sectors of our economy were at an all-time peak when the market collapsed in '29. Technology and industrial output were roaring, and many noted economists pronounced the market crash of '29 a "great buying opportunity."[3]

Look around the world today. Japan's economy, which came

dangerously close to a total meltdown in 1998, is teetering, with some of its biggest banks close to default. As I write this, the Japanese economy has gained a little ground, but on closer inspection you find it's because of government spending. Also, increased inventory orders in anticipation of Y2K may be providing some boost.

But other highly productive nations are in depression. Indonesia, the world's fourth-largest nation, has collapsed financially. So far, Brazil is barely surviving but only with the help of a massive International Money Fund bailout.

And Russia (reminiscent of the depression-era Germany) only distantly remembers its former status as a world superpower. In that once-powerful nation, government officials are telling workers that basic needs like food, oil, and electricity cannot be guaranteed anymore. "But," the ex-communist leaders promise, "you can count on having potatoes."[4]

One very sobering thought is to imagine what the world would be like today if Adolf Hitler had been able to grasp the reins of power in Germany and had assumed control over 18,000 nuclear weapons—and the missiles to deliver them. That is the scenario facing the world in Russia today. Political and military chaos usually follows economic chaos. The recent aggressive posture assumed by the U.S. only makes the rise of a dictator in Russia or China all the more possible.

America: Standing Alone in a Collapsing World?

So why has the U.S. been spared from the economic chaos? Or perhaps a better question might be, Why have we been spared *so far?* In *The Coming Economic Earthquake*, I speculated that the 1994 congressional elections would play a major role in the direction our economy would take. When the Republicans who ran on promises of tax cuts, welfare reform, and smaller government were swept into office, clearly we saw a return to "common sense" economics (at least in the short term).

I'm not trying to be partisan; if the tables had been turned, it could just as easily have been Democrats ousting Republican spenders. The point is that some fairly significant changes were made. We didn't get the anticipated tax cuts, but we did see Big Brother retreat in the face of lower government regulations, spending reductions, and a new pay-as-you-go welfare system that encouraged Americans to work. And, remember, Hillary Clinton's very expensive socialized health-care plan was defeated.

It is my belief that these relatively minor political changes sparked a much larger attitude change in our nation. As a result, our economy benefited from a new wave of optimism that spawned the largest expansion of any peacetime economy in history—one that, for the moment, seems "bulletproof" to any and all outside problems. But why?

One reason is the deflationary cycle we have experienced since the latter part of 1995. In *The Coming Economic Earthquake*, I noted that a deflationary period would restabilize our economy, but I also assumed (wrongly) that increasing federal deficits and falling revenues would lead to an inflationary spiral, as the government resorted to more credit.

Instead, thanks to the "bubble" that has isolated our economy from the rest of the world, we have reaped the benefits of lower prices on imported goods as other economies have shriveled; and, at the same time, we have experienced unparalleled growth in our own economy. This unanticipated windfall has kept overall prices low (even depressed), while real wages in America have actually increased. So far, we win; they lose.

Scales out of Balance

Unfortunately, one by-product of deflation is that we can no longer sell as many of our products to our trading partners; they simply do not have the money to spend. We have seen an unprecedented 53 percent rise in our trade deficit over the last two years.[5] As our exports decrease, the ripples of this contraction will eventually be felt in industries all across the country. In fact, according to *Fortune* magazine's annual listing of the largest U.S. public companies, profits for the Fortune 500 companies fell for the first time in seven years in 1998—a casualty of the economic crises in Asia, Russia, and Latin America.[6]

In 1998 the U.S. trade deficit soared to $169 billion, and prospects look even worse for 1999-2000.[7] But does the average American *really* care if corporate profits fall? After all, prices for imported goods continue to fall as other economies decline. That makes our kids' clothes cheaper, computers cheaper, and European vacations good deals. So why complain? In the short term, the U.S. consumers are the winners. Besides, in a "bubble" economy nothing seems to slow down the ride. The economy (and our stock market) has a shield around it that causes all bad news to bounce off. It seems that every time a company announces lower-than-anticipated earnings, the traders announce that it's a better buy and, ultimately, it soars even higher. So is there a penalty associated with our newfound prosperity? I think so.

Companies adjust their highest costpoint (salaries) based on profits or losses. If 20 percent of a company's employment is supported by exports and those exports fall by 50 percent, will the direct result be the reduction of 10 percent of its workforce? Not immediately. Companies will ride out short-term changes rather than displace employees, which is usually very costly. And it is very difficult to replace the trained labor force if the trend turns out to be temporary.

But if this negative export trend continues, further eroding foreign demand for U.S. products and services, Americans will face job layoffs on a major scale. One additional reality of too many imports and too few exports is that pressure-sensitive politicians try to curb foreign-made goods through trade barriers and tariffs. If our economy begins to slump, we could find ourselves in full-scale tariff wars; and tariff wars, history tells us, were one of the major economic factors that triggered the Great Depression.

Government Spending: Setting the Stage for Disaster

I also have to note that the spending cuts introduced by our politicians in 1994 are only *temporary*. Congress did *not* eliminate most programs; rather, they simply reduced the funding—meaning that a future Congress could reinstate all the old allocations and *more*. We've already seen a resurgence of pork-barrel politics as a result of the 1998 elections. And, as tax revenues continue to grow, in keeping with our incredible economic expansion, the temptation to further loosen the belt must be, for a politician, the ultimate siren song.

There is a lot of rhetoric being touted right now about *future* earnings. Just a few years ago, both Democrats and Republicans were predicting deficits as far as the eye could see. And now, with only two years of bloated tax revenues, they're working on spending plans that project endless surpluses, totaling an estimated $3 to $4 trillion over the next 15 years.[8]

Anyone familiar with past White House and Congressional Budget Office projections knows how good they are at estimating. Both have consistently underestimated spending while overestimating income. This practiced habit has led to deficits exceeding $300 billion in past years. When this economy turns down, we could be facing *huge* deficits, especially if the politicians lock in new spending programs. Rebuilding war-torn Eastern Europe won't be cheap by any standards.

More Income, Not Lower Spending

Contrary to what some politicians would have us believe, it is increased *income*, and not reductions in spending, that has kept the budget deficit down in recent years. It is important to understand that when the government owes interest to what are called intergovernmental accounts (Social Security Trust, Federal

Retirees Trust, Railroad Trust) these are *not* counted as a part of the annual deficit. In light of the projected surpluses, if these trust funds were properly accounted for, the overall *true deficit* would range from $80 billion in 1999 to $250 billion in 2009.[9]

If this economy stumbles, even slightly, we will be faced once again with overwhelming deficits that can easily pull us into the same mire one more time.

Social Security: On the Fault Line

Before I leave this area, I need to comment one more time on the Ponzi scheme known as the U.S. Social Security System. If Social Security were a private, regulated investment system, everyone involved probably would be indicted for securities fraud. It is a huge pyramid scheme in which the early participants are the winners and the latter are the losers. As more Americans age and live longer, the system consumes ever-greater amounts of money. Eventually the need for money will exceed all available funds.

But what about the Social Security Trust Fund, you say? Good question. Currently, Americans (more specifically, American baby boomers) pay more into Social Security than the system pays out annually. Theoretically, that surplus goes into the Social Security Trust Fund; but that's where the problems start.

Through a nifty accounting maneuver, the government shifts the "real money" into the General Revenue (counting it as income that can be spent) and issues a zero coupon bond (a letter of credit sold at a discount) to the Trust Fund. As a result, the Social Security "reserves" so often touted in Washington are really nothing more than a pile of government IOUs, slogging around in an impotent trust fund.

In the *Washington Post* George Hager said, "The entire Social Security Trust Fund, all $734 billion or so of it, fits readily in four ordinary, brown, accordion-style folders that one can easily hold in both hands. . . . Although they [the zero coupon bonds] look like something anyone could print on a home computer printer, they are official government documents, and the amounts on them are breathtaking. The largest bear a face value of nearly $51 billion."[10]

Hager adds, "The certificates are printed because four years ago then-Congressman Andy Jacobs wanted to silence the doubters."[11]

Who said there's no real Trust Fund? I'm sure the baby boomers sleep better at night now. When they are ready to retire, there won't be enough workers paying into the system to support them. To pay back the Social Security Trust Funds, the government will be forced to raise taxes, or borrow the money, or both! One estimate from the 1989 Social Security Administration Trust Board is that it will require a tax rate of approximately 87 percent to pay the bills. Therefore, Social Security must be reckoned as a huge potential economic liability.

Debt: Still the Main Problem

Of all the threats to our economy, from the worldwide financial troubles to our problems with Social Security, *debt* is still the 500-pound gorilla in our living rooms. Thirty years ago, we had $132 billion in *consumer debt* (i.e., credit cards, equity loans, autos). In 1998 that figure had exploded to $1.5 trillion, which translates into an average consumer debt load of $11,000 per family. Numbers like these may seem remote or irrelevant, but on our "Money Matters" radio broadcast I get the chance to talk with Christian families every day, and their real-life stories can be heartbreaking.

In any given month, we receive more than 100,000 calls to the radio program. Our typical caller is a married woman, with two children and a family income of $35,000 to $37,000 per year. In 1997 the majority of these callers were asking questions about investing: "Should I have a 401(k) or an IRA?" "Are mutual funds a good investment?"

What Happened to the Earthquake?

However, in 1998 we saw a radical shift in the questions asked. Most of our callers stopped asking about investing, even though the stock market continued to climb. Instead, most of them wanted to know what to do about their debt—specifically, credit card debt.

Our callers owed an average of between $7,000 and $10,000 in credit card debt, which, incidentally, parallels the national average of $11,000 in consumer debt per family. In essence, what many of these families were doing was investing in the stock market through retirement accounts and making up the differences in their living expenses by using credit cards for their everyday purchases.

All seemed well as long as their investments returned 25 to 30 percent. But with the market's volatility in 1998, many of these investors found their profits shrinking, and some even sustained serious losses. Stacked up against the 16 to 21 percent interest owed on their credit cards, many people found themselves in precarious financial positions.

The credit (lending) industry seems to have lost all pretense of common sense these days. Credit card companies are sending out applications en masse and soliciting virtually everyone who can breathe (college students, slow payers, no payers), and when their credit cards are maxed out, the companies oblige further with home equity loans (125 percent of equity), lines of credit, second mortgages, and total refinancing.

In an interesting sleight of hand, the total amount of consumer debt improved slightly in 1999—not because consumers used less credit but because they refinanced their consumer loans into their home mortgages. This works well in a growth cycle, but it bodes ill for the next downturn.

On a national scale, consumer debt has led to an unprecedented number of personal bankruptcies. Consumer bankruptcies are at an all-time high, which is a bad trend. If our brilliant politicians succeed in changing the bankruptcy law, it will be more difficult to go bankrupt. And, this will fix the bankruptcy problem about like issuing IOUs to the Social Security Trust Fund will fix Social Security. As a famous poet once said, "The madmen are running the insane asylum."

Since the rate of bankruptcies is growing in a *healthy* economy, when we do experience a downturn Americans will find themselves with huge personal debts and no way to pay them off. With the advent of liberal home equity loans, many families are upside-down in their home loans (owing more than they own). In tough times, the incentive to pay even these debts will wane. I wouldn't want to be a lender who is holding a $125,000 note on a $100,000 home in the next recession.

Debt's Not a Problem

Recently I had a prospective presidential candidate chide me for harping on the debt issue so much. "After all," he said, "we're handling the national debt just fine, and consumer debt helps the economy."

Well, I don't know about him, but I'll bet a few million average taxpayers could put to better use the $300 billion a year our government spends on interest payments. Do the couples who have their cars repossessed and the 50 percent who get divorced over debt problems feel better knowing they've helped the economy? I doubt it.

I just happen to believe debt does matter. Why? Because God's Word says it matters. *"The rich rules over the poor, and the borrower becomes the lender's slave"* (Proverbs 22:7).

On a personal level, large-scale consumer debt is a relatively new phenomenon. Forty years ago banks took a conservative approach to lending and issued credit only to people whose income or credit history indicated that they could repay the loan. Today, these same banks (along with countless retailers and credit card companies) happily provide credit to almost anyone with a pulse, target-marketing themselves even to financially naive college students and other low income or overextended borrowers.

Today 11 percent of all credit cards are held by 18- to 21-year-olds. But they represent 33 percent of all credit card debt, and 28 percent of them maintain a rollover balance each month.[12]

As long as the economy stays afloat, and borrowers can make the minimum payments, the game can go on. But if the downturn should catch the players unaware or unprepared, it's anyone's guess what could happen. In Japan, where consumers believed their prosperity was guaranteed, their economic woes have led to all-time highs in depression, divorce, and suicide. We now have a generation in America that seems to believe that prosperity is assured.

Another potential problem is that the average wage earner is also the government's primary provider. When the government needs more money (and, given the federal spending patterns, the government will always need more money), politicians raise our taxes or eliminate deductions in their insatiable appetite for our money. This translates into less spendable income for American workers, and less spending translates into fewer sales, which means less profits and fewer jobs and lower tax revenues, which means . . . well, you don't have to be a rocket scientist to see the potential for trouble.

Uncle Sam's Debt Problems

Of course, the consumer debt problem pales in comparison to our government's runaway debt. The federal debt can, and will, destroy our economy if it is not brought under control. Interest on the debt, even in a great economy, consumes 15 percent of total government income.[13]

It is interesting to note that of the $357 billion in government interest costs this year, $119 billion is owed to trust funds (Social Security and others) and will not be paid; nor will this amount be reflected in the government's deficit figures. Why? Because it is credited as an *asset*, not a liability. Go figure!

It seems that we have developed a strategy that *depends* on prosperity—a very bad assumption. Even if we could freeze spending right where it is now, the debt would eventually become unmanageable, simply because of the accumulating interest. It is like a bomb waiting to go off. The only question is, "How long is the fuse?" But since it won't be this year or next, few people seem to care anymore.

Dancing on the Deck

As I noted before, the spending cuts and other economic measures enacted by the 1994 and 1996 Congress bought us some time. Our economy has continued to expand, even in the face of a worldwide recession. How long the U.S. economy can carry the world is impossible to predict.

The trade deficit figures are staggering, as virtually every trading nation on earth dumps its products on our markets. The annualized trade deficit for 1999 at the time of this writing is expected to exceed $210 billion![14] As I have said, this is great for the price of imported merchandise but bad for jobs.

Today's investment climate continues to defy logic, especially for Internet-involved companies! For example, companies like Amazon.com have never made a profit to date, and last year they even posted a substantial loss. The Amazon securities prospectus states that the company does not expect to make a profit in the foreseeable future. This is normally not a commentary that is likely to attract investors; and yet, the stock continues to attract investors.

I personally made a modest investment in America Online stock so that I could have access to stockholders' information. At the time I bought the stock it was trading at about 400 times price-earnings ratio (PER). Within six weeks the PER was more than 600:1. In other words, if the stock price and company earnings were frozen, it would take more than 600 years to recover the investment! In the past, a good PER was considered to be about 11:1, yet the company's stock value continues to skyrocket! It's as if no amount of bad news can turn the tide of investor enthusiasm.

Actually, the phenomenon we're currently experiencing is not unlike the tulip-bulb mania that swept Europe in the 17th century. Today, these periods of market growth that have no statistical or reasonable explanations are commonly called "bubbles." A bubble happens when one sector of the economy—in this case, the technology-driven sector, which accounts for 90 percent of the Dow's profits—takes on a life of its own, carrying the overall market into the stratosphere.

The last time we saw such remarkable growth was during the 1928 stock market run-up and, prior to that, about 100 years earlier, when the industrial revolution catapulted railroad and communications stocks through the roof. All bubbles eventually burst, unless they can be deflated gradually. The stock market bubble of 1929 is commonly blamed for launching the Great Depression when it burst.

Are we in a similar situation right now? The parallels to the pre-Depression economy are eerily similar, from the unreal stock prices to the growing rumbles of trade disputes and tariff wars. Even more ominous than the economic indicators, though, are the psychological likenesses. As the Dow continues to climb, economic analysts assure us that "the fundamentals are sound," and many from generation X, who have never seen a major bear market, refuse to acknowledge that one is possible.

Just two days before the market crashed on October 22, 1929, Charles E. Mitchell, the chairman of National City Bank of New York, assured investors that "The industrial situation of the United States is absolutely sound, and our credit situation is in no way critical. . . . The markets generally are now in a healthy condition. . . . I know of nothing wrong with the stock market or with the underlying business and credit structure."[15]

The experts assured the public that the *Titanic* was unsinkable. Even after word got out that the great ship had hit an iceberg, passengers continued to dance on the decks. What was a floating chunk of ice compared to the marvel and ingenuity of modern shipbuilding?

We have at least two icebergs on the horizon: debt and Y2K. A shift in consumer confidence alone could throttle the economy, depending on a shift in the way the wind blows. Yet, we are still dancing on the decks; and we haven't even stopped to consider the potential impact of Y2K and the computer bug that, at least according to some observers, could sink the ship all by itself. Whether you agree or disagree, the year 2000 will bring some changes—but none that appear to be positive.

———

1. James K. Glassman and Kevin A. Hassett, "Stock Prices Are Still Far Too Low," *Wall Street Journal*, March 17, 1999.
2. *Financial Euphoria* (Whittle Books, 1990).
3. *New York Times*, July 1929.
4. CBS Broadcast Journalist David Dolan, speaking in Naples, Florida, on March 13, 1999.
5. Rich Miller, "US economy a bubble waiting to burst," *USA Today*, March 11, 1999, 1A.
6. *Winston-Salem Journal*, April 5, 1999, A3.
7. *USA Today*, March 11, 1999, 1A.
8. Congressional Budget Office, *The Economic and Budget Outlook Fiscal Years 2000–2009*, US Senate, January 29, 1999.
9. Ibid.
10. "Social Security? It's All Right Here; W. Va. Filing Cabinet Holds $734 Billion Funds IOUs," *Washington Post*, December 11, 1998, B1.
11. Ibid.

12. *Credit Counseling Debt Management Plan Analysis*, VISA USA, Inc., January 1999.
13. *The Economic and Budget Outlook Fiscal Years 2000–2009*, US Senate, January 29, 1999.
14. Beth Bolton, "January trade deficit hits record $17B," *USA Today*, March 19,1999.
15. *New York Times*, October 23, 1929.

2

A Bubble Economy?

Throughout much of the 17th century the city of Amsterdam served as the trading center for Western Europe. In 1634 a visitor to that city was able to purchase a silver cup for 60 florins, a suit of clothes for 80 florins, or 1,000 pounds of cheese (if the person liked goat cheese) for 120 florins. If the buyer was affluent and wanted to put down roots in the city, he could buy an 80-acre estate, complete with a gentleman's house and formal gardens, for about 4,000 florins.

Or, for just a little more money than the cost of the cup, the clothes, the cheese, and the home *combined*, the buyer could purchase an Admiral Liefken. The Admiral Liefken, whose price on the open market occasionally topped the 5,000-florin mark, was a particularly sought-after treasure. It weighed only a few ounces and could easily be slipped into your pocket; yet, to pursue this prize, traders regularly mortgaged land, homes, and even children—selling them as indentured servants—to own just one Liefken.

What, you might ask, is an Admiral Liefken? In contemporary

Europe, the Leifken is what most home owners use to adorn their flower gardens: a common *tulip*.

At one point in the 17th century, tulip bulbs were all the rage among market-savvy European investors. They were traded as speculative commodities, much like railroad stocks were during the 19th century or radio stocks in the 1920s and, more recently, like Internet stocks in our generation. Reading a textbook on 20th century economics, a student in the future year 2399 might regard today's investments in Yahoo! or eBay or America Online with the same puzzlement we feel about the Liefken. What made it such an astounding success?

For starters, it began as a scarce commodity. Small-time investors and other "riffraff" were effectively barred from owning the more precious varieties of Admiral Liefken, because prospective buyers had to demonstrate that they owned at least 12 acres of land on which they would plant a *single* bulb. By limiting availability, market regulators protected the Leifken's value by ensuring that it would not be overproduced.

(Today's South African diamond distributors have practiced much the same method of commodity control. It has been said that if all the diamonds just in the DeBeers Company vaults alone were suddenly dumped on the market, prices would plummet to only *dollars* per carat!)

More influential than price controls, however, was the *emotional mania* surrounding the buying and selling of these tulip bulbs. In the belief that their loans could be repaid easily from the profits of only a few trades in bulbs, families mortgaged lands and properties that had been held for generations to fund their tulip-bulb speculations. Across Europe, investors poured massive amounts of investment cash into Holland as the mania began to entice even the most skeptical buyers. Of course, common sense would have pointed out the poor *long-term value* in a perishable tulip bulb; yet speculation soared and "investment fever" overtook even the most pessimistic analysts.

A Bubble Economy?

Within a year, even the poorest Europeans were scraping together their meager savings to get in on "the opportunity of a lifetime." Envisioning riches beyond their wildest dreams, many peasants even sold the food they needed for their tables in exchange for a stake in the market.

Yet for rich and poor alike, bulb mania had drawbacks. One wealthy merchant who prided himself in his fine collection of tulip bulbs was delighted when a rare bulb arrived from Constantinople. To reward the sailor who carried the locked-and-sealed bulbs to Holland, the merchant offered him a fresh red herring for his breakfast and invited the seaman to wait in his study while he fetched the fish from the kitchen. While the merchant was gone, the sailor spied what he assessed as a fine, fat onion on the study desk. Since he dearly loved onions, he secretly slipped the orb into his pocket and looked forward to the taste it would add to his smoked-fish breakfast.

Later that morning, the merchant noticed that his rare *Semper Augustus,* a tulip bulb worth some 3,000 florins, was missing. After a frantic search failed to turn up the missing asset, the merchant remembered the sailor who had sat in his study and raced to the local tavern. He arrived just in time to watch the fellow polish off the last bite of what he described as the "most unusual onion he had ever tasted"! During the next few years the unlucky sailor had plenty of time to reflect on his meal (as he languished in the prisons of Amsterdam)—a meal that cost as much as the entire ship on which he had once served.

A similar fate befell a wealthy cobbler who had mortgaged his family business to speculate in tulip bulbs. After several successfully leveraged trades, the man acquired an exceptionally valuable specimen. He decided to sell the bulb at the market for cash, with which he planned to redeem his business and move comfortably into retirement.

Hurrying to the stable, he placed the bulb on the windowsill while he harnessed his horse for the journey. As he turned to pick up his saddle, he heard a crunching sound. You guessed it: The animal had eaten his investment!

Still another woeful tale is told of an English traveler who spied a highly unusual "root" lying in the conservatory of his Dutch cousin. An amateur botanist, the Englishman quickly dissected the attraction with his penknife, and he found himself consigned to a Dutch prison until his family could post a bond to pay 3,000 florins for his ill-considered experiment on his cousin's Admiral Liefken.

Such occasional misfortunes did nothing to deter the speculators from their perishable investments. Ordinary citizens, accustomed to earning only 200 florins a year, made fortunes of a lifetime almost overnight. Long considered the backbone of Europe's economy, trading in property and currency quickly fell into disfavor. Such investments merely *held* their value, but tulip bulbs were known to *double* or *triple* in value, often on a weekly basis.

Of course, as all investment manias eventually do, the tulip bulb "bubble" burst. When more prudent speculators realized the risks of using organic vegetation as security for loans far greater than real property values, they began to cash out their holdings. Others followed their lead, and it quickly became apparent that there was not enough money in all of Europe to redeem the speculations that had been made. Within a few weeks, *tulip mania* became *tulip malaise*. Fortunes disappeared in the blink of an eye, leaving only lawsuits, prison sentences, and sudden poverty in their wake.

Want to Buy Some Resort Property in Mississippi?

When France's Louis XIV died in 1715, the people's suppressed hatred of the dead monarch exploded; they recalled only Louis's extravagances and his cruelties at their expense. His effigies were torn down, and his statues were disfigured and pelted with rotten food. Louis's name was synonymous with selfishness and oppression.

A Bubble Economy?

The heir to Louis's throne was a child of about 7 years of age, so the Regent, Philippe II, Duke of Orleans, assumed the reins of an impoverished government. No man felt more deeply than the Duke about the deplorable state of his country, but few men were less suited to run the country.

He disdained manual labor, he disliked any daily routine, he signed official documents without properly examining them, and he entrusted to others the responsibilities he should have carried himself. In other words, he abdicated his role in the governing of France, and others took advantage.

Duke de St. Simon, financial advisor to the Duke of Orleans, believed nothing could save the country from revolution, except a bold and dangerous financial remedy: France should declare national bankruptcy. Of course, others foresaw that such an action would have led to total anarchy across the country, so it was discouraged. Instead, the French government began to recoin its currency and, to the chagrin of all who lived within its borders, it was depreciated by about one-fifth.

In the midst of this financial confusion, Scottish banker and writer John Law appeared on the scene. In England, Law's suggestions for trade and revenue reforms (including a national bank and the issuance of paper money without a gold reserve to guarantee its value) had been rejected soundly. He had been run out of England and Scotland under threat of being hanged!

The discredited financier suddenly found himself in a more favorable position in France. At that time, France's national debt was about 3 billion *livres* (today, they would be called francs). The government had an annual income of only 145 million *livres,* with expenses of 142 million *livres.* Simple arithmetic shows they had a surplus of only 3 million *livres* to pay toward the interest on their 3 billion *livres* debt—hardly enough to keep the government solvent.

John Law convinced the Duke that it would be in the interest of the French government to print new money on paper, as opposed to using only hard currency in gold or silver. The Duke himself thought this to be a great plan, since in fact it sounded like a way to create new money out of thin air. The privately owned Bank of France was chartered to print paper currency, although the government had only one-half a *livre* for every new note printed. Care to guess who was given ownership of the new bank? The Duke's enterprising protégé, John Law!

Later that year, in order to promote the bank's interests, Law convinced the Duke to set up the Mississippi Delta Land Company, whose stock was held by the Bank of France. The company had an exclusive monopoly for marketing the land and assets of French colonies in the New World: Mississippi and Western Louisiana. It was widely rumored throughout Europe that Mississippi was literally sinking under the weight of gold, and the Mississippi Delta Land Company was going to mine and export that gold back to France.

Law advertised that Louisiana was a land full of mountains of gold and silver. Stories were told of an emerald rock that sat on the Arkansas River. The acceptance of such outrageous claims at face value is puzzlingly similar today to the purchase of many of the Internet stocks by wide-eyed buyers.

The following year, the Duke made Law his controller general of finances, and Law's bank took control over most of the national debt and the national administration of revenue. Then, he merged his huge stock company with his national bank, and both speculators and small investors excitedly bought stock in the expanded operation.

Law, the Duke, and the Mississippi Delta Land Company promised returns of 120 percent interest per year, so, obviously, the plan was a huge hit with French speculators who were used to making only 1½ to 2 percent interest on their investments. Within six months after issue, shares in the Mississippi Delta Land Company grew from about 100 *livres* per share to 5,000 *livres* per share. Then, in the next two years, the rest of France's colonial trade (in the Indies, China, and Africa) was consolidated with the Mississippi Delta Land Company as the Compaigne des Indes. An economic bubble had developed and the entire country wanted in on the deal.

The Duke ordered that 300,000 new shares from the Mississippi Delta Land Company should be issued at the new price of 5,000 *livres* per share. Because of this rapid inflation in the value of the shares, more and more people clamored to buy them. The street surrounding John Law's home was jam-packed full of people every morning; the throngs often exceeded 15,000 at once. Sometimes, the crowds were so great that people were crushed against the stone walls and died in the midst of share trading.

In order for speculators to stay close to John Law, they clamored for rental space on his street, the Rue de Quincampoix; apartment rentals soared from about 1,000 *livres* per year to 16,000 *livres* immediately.

The Smartest Man in the World

Of course, by this time, John Law was thought to be the smartest man in the world and the Duke of Orleans one of the wisest leaders. After all, the government of France had the exclusive franchise on issuing shares in the Mississippi Delta Company, and the billions of *livres* it was collecting were going to help pay off the national debt and ensure prosperity for the entire population. The French people were ecstatic over the new wealth they were accumulating in their ever-increasing shares.

Buying mania set in. Prices for shares in the Mississippi Delta Land Company often rose 10 to 20 percent in *an hour*, making common cobblers wealthy. Commoners with the courage to speculate were now able to buy carriages and castles.

One servant, sent by his master to sell 250,000 shares in the Mississippi Delta Land Company at the going rate of 8,000 *livres* per share, reached the square, only to find the shares were worth 10,000 *livres* each. So, the servant pocketed the difference of half-a-billion *livres,* bought himself a new set of clothes and a new carriage, and promptly made his way to another country in Europe!

As in all cases, someone was ready to throw water on the fire to put out the party. A well-known, conservative banker, Monsignor Marshall Villars, let it be known that he thought the Mississippi Delta Land Company was a fraud. One day, while passing John Law's house and observing the enormous swell of speculators shouting and waving their purchase money, Mr. Villars signaled his driver to stop and shouted from the carriage window that the people were stupid, that there was no value in the shares they were accumulating. The crowd assaulted him, pelting his carriage with fruits, vegetables, and wine bottles. After that, Monsignor Villars kept his opinions to himself!

In France, industrial production rose to match this new prosperity. Homes were built in every direction surrounding Paris. Restrictions on credit were lifted in accordance with Law's economic theories, and people who had never been allowed to have credit before were now extended credit far beyond their ability to repay through their ordinary incomes. Not to worry, the bankers said; their creditworthiness was based on the *speculative wealth* that was being made in the Mississippi Delta Land Company. With little hard currency available, their shares were being paid for with the new paper money. Prosperity abounded, as long as people trusted John Law.

Nobody ever thought to mention that not even one ounce of gold had been dug out of the ground in Mississippi and shipped back to France. After all, the real product of the Mississippi Delta Land Company was shares in the company, not gold. France's new wealth was the envy of the entire continent. Virtually everyone believed John Law to be the smartest financier who had ever walked the earth.

To his credit, Law did not personally exploit his land schemes other than buying himself a castle, which he said was for the purpose of selling shares. The castle had a large courtyard, allowing 15,000 to 25,000 people per day to bid on the new and existing shares in the Mississippi Delta Land Company.

John Law had created wealth out of thin air, and no Parisian was willing to be denied. Eventually bankers, financiers, and the wealthy families of Europe succumbed to the frenzy. They snapped up the new shares as soon as they were offered. Noble French ladies would beguile their way into dinners with Law and then pester him with pleas to sell them stocks, until he refused all dinner invitations. Royalty and justices alike tried every trick to get to Law. One magistrate even went so far as to have him hauled into court, just to bully him from the bench to sell him a few shares.

But not everyone was so naive. A few foreign traders, seeing the foolishness of all the speculations, traded their paper for gold and silver coins, which they promptly loaded into carts, covered with manure, and smuggled out of France. Eventually, the French banking community also realized there was too much paper money in circulation with respect to hard currency. So, the banks limited conversion of paper-to-coins to no more than 500 *livres* per individual, per month, trying to prevent a massive run against paper money. A crack in the wall of prosperity began to develop.

As stockholders began questioning the value of the Mississippi Delta Land Company shares, ships were filled with enthusiastic "miners," who sailed from France under the pretense of going to America. A few hundred miles down the coast, these "miners" were put ashore, where they promptly sold all their mining tools and made their way back to Paris where, once again, they were hired as prospectors and miners by the company to repeat the process. The grand scheme had grown beyond the limits of propriety.

In an effort to support the highly inflated paper money, by 1720 France forbade ownership of gold and jewels. Gold and silver were being confiscated by the government so the banks would have resources to back its paper currency. Servants betrayed their masters out of "patriotism" and for large rewards. Hoarding just two ounces of gold could get the owner a prison sentence of 10 years or more.

Well-informed speculators discovered that the gold mines in Mississippi were nonexistent. Men who had gone to the Delta to investigate came back and reported that no gold of any kind had been found in Mississippi. Shares in the Mississippi Delta Land Company were trading for as high as 20,000 *livres* per share when those who had discovered the real story began dumping their shares at huge profits. This touched off a selling frenzy, and in less than six weeks stockholders couldn't give away their shares in the Mississippi Delta Land Company.

At that point, more than 2.5 billion *livres* in paper currency were in circulation, backed by gold and silver reserves of only 1,000 *livres*. Where had France's gold and silver gone? It had found its way out of the country to other, saner parts of Europe.

The Duke of Orleans' "funny money" was immediately devalued at the rate of 10:1. The two most admired men in France, the Duke and his financier, John Law, quickly became the two most hated men in the country. In disgrace, Law fled for his life once again. Until his death, he lived in Venice, where he supported himself as a gambler.

After the Mississippi Land Scheme failed in 1721, France's debt stood at 3.1 billion *livres* and the government was, for all intents and purposes, totally bankrupt. Both the Regency and the idea of a national bank were totally discredited. When the bubble burst, it made quite a mess![1]

A Bubble Economy?

1. Charles Mackay, *Extraordinary Popular Delusions and the Madness of Crowds* (New York: John Wiley & Sons, Inc., 1995).

3

"Sensible"
Speculation?

A current speculator might argue, "I'd never do something as silly as speculate in tulip bulbs." On the Internet, I found a list of the world's greatest "bubbles" and the "pins" that popped them. All of them seemed to be "reasonable" at the time.

- **Real Estate**—Three hundred thirty years before the birth of Jesus, a speculative land boom in ancient Greece went bust after a lengthy period of high profits. It is said that the people who bought in last (when prices were at their highest) could have recouped their initial investment (not counting inflation) only if they had lived another 1,000 years. That's how long it took for Athens' real estate to reach those prices again!

- **Banking**—In the 1770s, the British banking crisis was a result of unrealistically high property values, overextended banks, and a booming stock market. Experts later blamed it on a "herd mentality" among investors. Scotsman Charles MacKay recognized the danger of following the "herd" in 1841, when he wrote, "Men, it has been said, think in herds; it will be seen that they go mad in herds, while they only recover their senses slowly, and one by one."

- **Government Projects**—Two years later, in France, Credit Mobilier collapsed, taking the fortunes of many common Frenchmen, along with major financial institutions. It had been endorsed by Napoleon III and produced many of the landmarks and wide boulevards you see when visiting Paris today. How could the average investor have guessed it was not a solid investment? After all, the government was behind it!

- **International Trade**—In the early 1700s, the South Sea Company planned to pay off the British government's debts through trading with Spanish America. People to whom the government owed large portions of its national debt were persuaded to swap for shares in the venture. As stock value climbed from £100 to £1,000, people invested in every impossible project remotely connected to the company. Profits never materialized; there were no funds to maintain projects. The national debt was not paid off. Investors across the Empire were wiped out. Jonathan Swift parodied the event in his story of *Gulliver's Travels*.

- **Commodities Speculation**—The Indian Cotton Boom was a result of the Civil War. American cotton was being made into ready-to-wear uniforms, and demand was so high that cotton prices in the U.S. have never again reached that price. Speculators in Bombay invested incredible sums in Indian cotton, but at the end of the Civil War prices collapsed, and so did India's national economy.

- **Stock Market Investing**—In 1866 a well-known discount house collapsed in London. Within a month, the Royal Bank of Scotland had fallen, and panic spread all the way to America. A major part of the problem was investor panic, fueled by a brand new invention: the ticker tape provided almost instant announcements of every downturn. And, according to John Kenneth Galbraith, Wall Street's Great Crash of 1929 had its causes "all in the speculative orgy that preceded it." In the following three years, the Dow lost 89 percent of its value. The failure of a bank in Vienna is generally credited with causing our crash; and in a domino effect stocks in Belgium, Canada, France, Great Britain, and Holland lost 50 to 85 percent of their value.

- **Precious Metals**—The Hunt brothers of Texas almost cornered the silver market in January of 1980. But less than three months later, the speculative market collapsed and the family lost more than $1.8 billion. Many other investors were caught up in the excitement of accumulating precious metals. The collapse of silver pushed gold ever higher.

  The Alderdice brothers in Fort Lauderdale, Florida, founded the International Gold Bullion Exchange to sell gold coins worldwide. Then they began selling speculative options. Eventually, they offered purchasers the company vault for the storage of their gold, showing pictures of the gold the company was already storing. When the *Wall Street Journal* became suspicious and stopped running their advertisements, their business began to fall apart. Federal investigators raided the company's headquarters, and in the vault they found—you guessed it—only pieces of wood carved and painted to look like gold ingots. Shortly thereafter, one brother was murdered and the other brother was sentenced to enough time in prison to punish both brothers.[1]

Nothing New Under the Sun

Economic bubbles are not new; they occur whenever euphoria sets into a market and trading prices ignore the actual value of the commodity or the company involved. If we look at the current

U.S. economy (and particularly our stock market), it is quite possible to believe that we are developing another bubble, as the following so vividly illustrates.

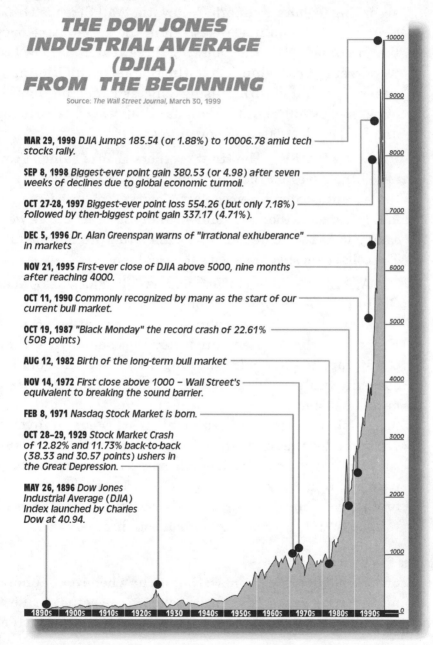

THE DOW JONES INDUSTRIAL AVERAGE (DJIA) FROM THE BEGINNING

Source: *The Wall Street Journal,* March 30, 1999

MAR 29, 1999 *DJIA jumps 185.54 (or 1.88%) to 10006.78 amid tech stocks rally.*

SEP 8, 1998 *Biggest-ever point gain 380.53 (or 4.98) after seven weeks of declines due to global economic turmoil.*

OCT 27-28, 1997 *Biggest-ever point loss 554.26 (but only 7.18%) followed by then-biggest point gain 337.17 (4.71%).*

DEC 5, 1996 *Dr. Alan Greenspan warns of "irrational exhuberance" in markets*

NOV 21, 1995 *First-ever close of DJIA above 5000, nine months after reaching 4000.*

OCT 11, 1990 *Commonly recognized by many as the start of our current bull market.*

OCT 19, 1987 *"Black Monday" the record crash of 22.61% (508 points)*

AUG 12, 1982 *Birth of the long-term bull market*

NOV 14, 1972 *First close above 1000 – Wall Street's equivalent to breaking the sound barrier.*

FEB 8, 1971 *Nasdaq Stock Market is born.*

OCT 28–29, 1929 *Stock Market Crash of 12.82% and 11.73% back-to-back (38.33 and 30.57 points) ushers in the Great Depression.*

MAY 26, 1896 *Dow Jones Industrial Average (DJIA) Index launched by Charles Dow at 40.94.*

1890s | 1900s | 1910s | 1920s | 1930 | 1940s | 1950s | 1960s | 1970s | 1980s | 1990s

10000 · 9000 · 8000 · 7000 · 6000 · 5000 · 4000 · 3000 · 2000 · 1000 · 0

"Sensible" Speculation?

Let me give you some interesting statistics as of June 1, 1999.

- There are approximately 4,400 stocks traded on the NAS-DAQ market, but only 26 of these companies now account for almost 95 percent of the gains among NASDAQ stocks over the last year and one-half.
- Twenty-one of 26 companies whose Internet stocks have driven the market up are actually losing money rather than making money.
- Of the Internet stocks traded on the NASDAQ market, 1,300 have lost a composite 6.8 percent.

This suggests that a very narrow market is developing among technology stocks—when only 26 companies' stocks account for 95 percent of the gain, and 21 of those 26 companies are not making a profit! Even worse, when you read the prospectuses of some of these companies, they say that not only have they not made money but also they do not anticipate making money in the near future. And, according to some of the reports, they may *never* be able to make a profit!

In an article by David Dreman in *Forbes,* March 1999, he said, "With hindsight, the market in 1929 was overpriced prior to the 1929 crash, when it traded at a Price Earnings Ratio (PER) of 22 [to 1]. What we are witnessing today is a full-scale *industromania* of the sort seen in the tulip-buying frenzy of 1636, or the South Sea Island bubble of 1721. The bubble is visible almost everywhere in the market, but it is most conspicuous in the technology stocks. Twenty-five large technology issues accounted for 93 percent (the percentages will change depending on who you read) of the NASDAQ's 40 percent growth over the last year and 100 percent of its 5.8 percent gain to date, as of March 1999. There are 4,460 NASDAQ stocks that were down 3 percent in 1998. 'But don't worry about these statistics,' say the bull advocates. 'We're entering a new era...'"[2]

Have we ever heard that one before! I have to admit, though, that I had to look long and hard to find articles suggesting that this current market is overvalued. As happened to Marshall Villars in the Mississippi Delta Land Scheme, people who are trading high and making lots of money don't want to hear the detractors. In fact, they will pelt them with eggs and tomatoes if they speak out.

Quoting David Dreman again, "What makes bubbles possible is that human beings are not good statistical processors. For instance, we tend to forget that red-hot new issues, whether they are computer-leasing or semiconductor stocks in the 1960s or PC companies in the 1980s, have provided horrendous returns on average."[3]

Dreman notes that a study of new issues between 1970 and 1990 showed a median return of -45 percent for five years. But, he says, "people often ignore the averages while focusing entirely on the memorable exceptions like Microsoft."[4] And this is true. People tend to put losers out of their minds and focus on winners. Right now, more people are "winning" than "losing," so it is very difficult to deter people from pursuing loss in search of profit.

Anatomy of a Bubble

People love the excitement of a bubble. I recall seeing it on a much smaller scale when I was in my late 20s, working at the Space Center in Florida. A promoter, Glen Turner, started a company in central Florida called "Dare To Be Great." The company did not sell any products, although it did have a cassette tape motivational message program. The real purpose behind the company was selling the idea that you too could "dare to be great."

The concept was relatively simple: Investors signed up in the program for a fee of $5,000, for which they got a set of "Dare To Be Great" cassette tapes. But this fee also permitted them to sign up their friends and family for $5,000 each. Of that amount, $2,500 went back to the company, and $2,500 went to the recruiter. So the arithmetic was pretty simple: If you signed up two people, you got all your money back. If you signed up three people, you were $2,500 ahead.

I attended several of their sales meetings, and it was clear that what motivated the promoters was personal greed, rather than the belief that their prospects could be "great." Most of the people who signed up were from average working families. They had never made $2,500 a month in their lives. Yet they were easily convinced that by selling to at least one of their friends or family members every month they would be able to net $2,500.

At their big meetings, Mr. Turner told his story about being the stuttering, handicapped child of a sharecropper, who raised himself to millionaire status by believing in himself. To the chorus of 3,000 hooting and cheering attendees, Turner would shout and clap as he called twin midgets onto the stage. With great emotion, they shared with the audience that if *they* could make millions of dollars by "daring to be great," then *anybody* could make millions of dollars. Even with all the hype, I was far too conservative to buy into the scheme. But at the end of the presentation, I was amazed to see more than 500 people scramble to pay $5,000 of their hard-earned money for a set of cassette tapes and the right to "fleece" their friends.

"So," you might ask, "what's that got to do with the bubble economy?" In fact, it was a microversion of what can happen on a macroscale economically. The "Dare To Be Great" program grew to enormous proportions. Eventually, it attracted the attention of the Securities and Exchange Commission, which ultimately shut it down as a pyramid scheme. But this was not until tens of thousands of people had put $5,000 or more into the "Dare To Be Great" coffers.

How a Bubble Develops and Its Value Is Measured

I am always amazed how a program can start with little or no economic value and expand beyond all norms. When it happens on a large scale, the traditional rules for making investments, such as price-earnings ratios (PERs), and potential future growth and intrinsic value seem irrelevant. When this happens, a program, or more correctly a scheme, can bypass all risk-evaluating norms. We can't always count on the professionals to recognize for us when the bubble has burst. For instance, the following ad was published by a major brokerage house the day after the stock market crash, on October 25, 1929.[5]

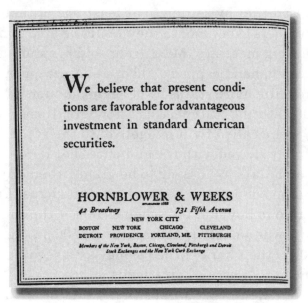

I wonder what the Wall Street wizards will be advising us the day after it all starts to come apart this time.

Underserving but Overvalued

As Mr. Dreman noted earlier, the average PE ratio just before the Great Crash of 1929 was 22:1. Today the average PE ratio— even on the Dow—is 32:1. Some of the ratios in the NASDAQ market defy logic; they are almost at infinity. Here are some interesting statistics to at least think about, quoted from *Barron's* magazine.

"Sensible" Speculation?

THEN

- In 1929 Radio Corporation of America (RCA) stock sold for a PE of 85:1; it dropped to 36:1 in 1929 before the Great Crash.

- Xerox sold for 256:1 (256 times its earnings) in 1961, and then by '68 had slid to 74:1.

- Apple Computer was 144:1 in 1981; it fell to 28:1 by 1988.[6]

NOW

- As of this writing, America Online stock sells at a PE of 577:1.

- Yahoo! sells at a ratio of 569:1.

- Charles Schwab Internet is selling for a ratio of 170:1.

- eBay is selling at a ratio of 3,324:1!

This spread between price and earnings leaves a long way to fall when investors start trying to cash out.

The Unbalance of Trade

There are several factors that indicate this booming economy is a bubble (in my opinion).

- The trade deficit has soared to an all-time record of $230 billion.

- Yet it does not seem to effect our economy whatsoever. If anything, it looks like we have improved, irrespective of the facts.

- The Federal Reserve reported that consumer borrowing climbed almost $13 billion in January 1999 and continues to climb today.

- Our personal savings rate, as measured by the Commerce Department, fell to -.7 percent of income (negative seven-tenths of 1 percent), the lowest level since 1933 and down sharply from 2.1 percent in 1997. (David Wise, chief economist at Standard and Poor, said something that I believe strongly: People are living too far beyond their means.)

- Federal Reserve Chairman Alan Greenspan has been cautioning investors for more than two years that the stock market's too high. (But any investor who heeded his warning back in December 1996 that "irrational exuberance" was driving prices would have missed out on a more than 60 percent rise in the Dow. Isn't that amazing?)

- The year 1999 was supposed to be a year of recovery for the whole global economy, but it hasn't turned out that way. In Asia, Japan's economy is still struggling to recover after its worst recession since World War II.

- In Europe, hopes for an economic pickup as a result of the new currency, the Euro, are now fading, and Europe is going to have a very slow year, according to former U.S. Treasury Secretary Robert Rubin.

- In Latin America, the region's largest economy (Brazil) is set to suffer an even sharper downturn this year, after a crisis that saw its currency plummet more than 35 percent last year. Economist Joseph Petry of Solomon Smith Barney thinks Brazil's economy will shrink another 5 percent in 1999.

- "Twenty percent of all U.S. exports should be going to Latin America. But all of Latin America is in the doldrums."[7]

- "The unprecedented divergence between the strong U.S. economy and the enfeebled rest of the world cannot continue."[8]

What comes to mind at this point is Robert Sobel's article in the February 1999 issue of *Barron's*. He stated, "Remember the old story about the two traders who kept selling a case of sardines to each other, raising the price each time—a surefire profit on every trade. Then one decided to sample the contents and found them inedible. 'Well, what did you expect?' asked his colleague. 'They were for trading, not for eating.'"[9]

And so it may be for some of today's Internet stocks. Mr. Sobel briefly describes other bubbles that have developed in the past. I'm sure those people thought they were pretty smart too.

- In 18th-century England, a company was set up to manufacture radish oil, which had no known use.

- Another was organized for carrying on an undertaking of great advantage, but no one was to know what that was.

- "The cry in the market," wrote a newspaper in 18th-century England, "was, for goodness sake, let us subscribe to something, we don't care what it is."

- During the 1830s, shares in canals and eastern railroads sold like hot Internet IPOs today but ultimately dropped out the bottom.

- Likewise, in the 1920s, there were Internet-style manias in radio, motion pictures, automobiles, and aviation.[10]

So there is one thing of which we can be certain: If this is a bubble developing in our economy and in our stock market, it is not a new phenomenon; it is one that has been around for a long, long while.

What If It's Not a Bubble After All?

On the other side, an article in *Barron's* reported on Goldman Sachs analyst Abbey Joseph Cohen's speech to her alumni group at Cornell University: Cohen asserted that the Standard and Poor's operating profits will be higher in 1999 and 2000, and the economy is doing just fine, thank you—creating new decent paying jobs, bolstering consumer confidence, and continuing to dissipate all despair. "The economy is in absolutely terrific condition and, notwithstanding the huge rise in stock prices since September, stock prices should continue to rise in the months ahead," she asserted. I think we should all pray that she is, in fact, correct and this is not a bubble developing in our economy.[11]

It is an interesting statistic that more Americans now own stock than ever before in our history. According to the Aden Research Group, nearly 50 percent of all U.S. households now own stock, compared to less than 20 percent 20 years ago. That means three things.

1. There is more money available to put in the stock market, giving it much greater power and more sustained strength.
2. The U.S. economy is much more vulnerable to shifts in the stock market, both up and down, and as a result of a major downshift, more American families are going to be in crisis.
3. About half of all Americans don't own stocks; therefore, they are not participating in this "boom" market.

There is another side in this argument. An article entitled "If This Is a Bubble, It Sure Is Hard to Pop," in the March 30, 1999 issue of the *Wall Street Journal,* points out the following two things.

• Yale University economist Robert Shiller says, "Hints of a bubble about to burst are everywhere. Online trading is turning personal computers into slot machines." But, according to naysayers, they've all been pointing this out for years, and so far they've been spectacularly wrong. The manager of the world's largest mutual fund, Fidelity Magellan Fund, bet billions that the bull market was over at the end of 1995. The Dow Jones Industrial Average has doubled since then, and he is no longer at Fidelity.

Professor Shiller declared in July 1996: "We appear to be flying in the wrong direction, and the correction could be substantial and lasting." Since that time, the Dow has risen 87 percent. And, as I pointed out earlier, the Industrial Average has climbed another 60 percent since Federal Reserve Chairman Alan Greenspan uttered the most memorable phrase of his career in December 1996, referring to the market's "irrational exuberance."

- Another quote from Vanguard Group mutual fund investor John Brennan: "We've had a run in the stock market that is unprecedented. You have to scratch your head and say, 'Is there something fundamentally different?' You start from the position of great skepticism, but it's conceivable there is a new paradigm developing."[12]

Overstaying Your Welcome

Before I close this chapter, let me give you a few more things to think about. These are sobering warnings that we may be winding up a ticking time bomb rather than defusing the situation.

- The cover story of the January 22, 1999 issue of *USA Today* had this quote. "'I look for 10,000 on the Dow by the end of the year without any trouble,' says Greg Ashwill, a traffic reporter for an Anchorage radio station."[13] The Dow Jones Industrial Average has exceeded 11,000 and continues to climb as of this writing. Veteran market watchers warn that such unbridled confidence is very dangerous.

- "This market has never been higher, faster or louder," says James Grant of Grant's *Interest Rate Observer*. "To me, the risks weighed against potential rewards have never been greater."[14]

- Now I'll risk one more quote (though you may consider me a rainstorm in a cotton candy festival). "The other aspect that creates a panic is man's greed. Part of man's optimism runs wild. He is so sure that things can only get better that, in effect, he 'borrows from tomorrow' to finance today, forgetting that tomorrow has to be financed too. The system might work if the borrowing were constant, but as greed or optimism grows geometrically and the borrowing for today gets bigger and bigger, so tomorrow's debt grows disproportionately and indigestibly. In the past in the U.S., the outcome of all this has always been panic. Odds are that it will be the same in the future, unless the form of government changes. For only in a total dictatorship are panics eliminated."[15]

Can You Afford to Be Wrong?

I personally believe that this bubble will burst. Why? Because I do not believe we have entered a new paradigm where value and earnings no longer matter. Obviously, we are going to hear hype from the media because, in large part, the hype has been winning. The market is up and the economy is booming—in spite of a worldwide recession.

The question is, can you afford to assume that this unbridled optimism will continue? If not, then you need to look at where your assets are invested and not have the major portion at risk.

Today's "tulip.com mania" centers around high-tech stocks—specifically, Internet stocks—and, to a lesser degree, technical stocks in general. To historians and students of America in the 1920s, the current wave of speculation bears a remarkable resemblance to the "sky's-the-limit" thinking of the years leading to the Great Depression. Times were good, prosperity was everywhere, and optimism abounded—right up until that fateful Thursday in October of 1929.

Are we on a parallel course? Most investment advisors, particularly the younger ones, think not. Today's computer programs, they say, allow us to analyze trends more accurately than ever, and our modern monetary and communications systems work to forestall yesteryear's desperate runs. But as billionaire Bernard Baruch pointed out, "In the midst of a mania, even sober minds begin to believe that the gains will never cease."

When asked how he knew when to pull his millions out of the market while so many others were still in a buying frenzy, Baruch answered: "When the local shoeshine man began to give me tips on which stocks to buy, I knew it was time to sell."[16]

So, look around you. In today's investment world, the shoeshine men have been replaced by day traders who quit their jobs as grocery clerks to speculate in stocks over the Internet.

———

1. Charles Mackay, *Extraordinary Popular Delusions and the Madness of Crowds* (New York: John Wiley, & Sons, Inc., 1995).
2. David Dreman, *Forbes*, March 1999.
3. Ibid.
4. Ibid.
5. Reprinted, Harry D. Schultz, *Panics and Crashes and How You Can Make Money Out of Them* (New Rochelle, NY: Arlington House, 1972).
6. Robert Sobel, "Mania Milestones," *Barron's* magazine, February 22, 1999 (an Internet citing).
7. Rich Miller, "U.S. Economy a Bubble Waiting to Burst," *USA Today*, March 11, 1999, A1.
8. *The Bank Credit Analysts*, February 1999 edition.
9. Sobel, "Mania Milestones," *Barron's*.
10. Ibid.
11. "If This Is a Bubble, It Sure Is Hard to Pop," *Wall Street Journal*, March 30, 1999, A1.
12. Ibid., A1.

13. Gary Strauss, "Investor Frenzy 'Little guy' on Wall Street goes running with the bulls," *USA Today*, January 22, 1999, 1A.
14. "Trading Up a Storm," *Grant's Interest Rate Observer*, November 20, 1998.
15. Harry D. Schultz, *Panics and Crashes, and How You Can Make Money Out of Them* (New Rochelle, NY: Arlington House, 1972), 185.
16. Robert Sobel, *Panic on Wall Street* (New York: E.P. Dutton, 1988).

Y2K: Economic Fallout
from the Big Computer Bug

When I wrote *The Coming Economic Earthquake* nearly a decade ago, there was no mention of Y2K in the media. I had read nothing about a "computer bug," a "millennium bug," or any other problems associated with the dawn of the 21st century. Incredible as it sounds, according to some "techno-watchers," this electronic dark horse—virtually unknown to the public at large until the past year or two—now threatens to spell the "end of the industrialized world, as we know it."

For the readers who are still in the dark about Y2K—and according to most news polls that group includes some 30 percent of American adults—the problem is that many older computer programs and digital controllers read only the last two digits of a year code. Since the majority of programs written in this century, as well as the digital controllers, assume a "19" in front of the two digits they read, it is assumed that a date code containing only "00" for the year 2000 will be interpreted as "1900." Thus, the year 2000 noted only as "00" will be mistaken for the year 1900.

As a result, we are told, many computer programs and digital controllers will malfunction or break down, possibly threatening such basic services as electricity, water, and transportation.

How bad will the problem be? The predictions vary. Almost everyone agrees that we will see some disruption in our day-to-day activities, perhaps along the lines of the breakdowns we experience after a major storm. And even though authors like Michael Hyatt (*The Millennium Bug: How to Survive the Coming Chaos*) warn of the potential for months-long power outages, bank failures, and crippled or absent police protection, others take a less drastic view.

Christian Computing magazine's Steve Hewitt, for instance, says that any computer-related problems that arise on January 1, 2000 will likely be fixed in short order and that the greatest danger we face is the possibility that millions of misinformed people will panic.

For my part, I'm somewhere between the two extremes. I do not think we will see the "end of western civilization," but I do believe the Y2K scoffers are in for a fairly significant surprise, at least in the first few days of 2000 and the first few months of the new millennium. Even after the physical disruptions are past, we still will have to contend with the longer-term concern of the economic fallout from Y2K.

The statistical probability of altering millions of lines of computer code and not having latent "bugs" is virtually impossible. How these bugs will manifest themselves will be known only after January 1, 2000. Anyone who has ever modified or upgraded an operating computer system should have no illusions as to the problems that can occur. We nearly always have hidden bugs when we upgrade our ministry system, even after exhaustive pretesting.

The biggest potential difficulty associated with Y2K, however, is not in the United States. After reviewing every piece of available data to date, including the House and Senate Committee hearings,[1] I am convinced that, except for public panic, our outages of power and communications systems and shortages will be sporadic, irritating, and frustrating, but not life threatening.

However, with our dependence on foreign oil, materials, and products, the economic impact can be devastating, because major parts of the industrialized world are delinquent in taking the Y2K problem seriously, and many have simply started too late and do not have the resources to effect Y2K compliance. Therefore, I have concluded that their laxness will severely impact the world's economy in the year 2000.

Y2K HOW BAD? Over 200 Y2K professionals from business, government, and military sectors anticipate the severity of Y2K's impact:

84% At least a 20% drop in the stock market and some business bankruptcies.

66% An economic slowdown, a rise in unemployment, and some isolated social incidents.

56% A mild recession, isolated infrastructure and supply problems, and some runs on banks.

34% A strong recession, local social disruptions, and many bankruptcies.

26% Political crises within the U.S., regional supply and infrastructure disruptions, regional social disruptions.

10% U.S. suffers depression (or worse), financial markets collapse, crippled infrastructure, local martial law.

Source: Washington DC Year 2000 Group (www.wdcy2k.org/survey/) reported in *New Man* magazine, January–February 1999

From a practical perspective, these Y2K-related inventory and supply problems make the recession scenario I outlined in Chapter 1 (and for that matter in *The Coming Economic Earthquake* book) a real possibility. Even without Y2K, our economy is stretching the historical limits of the economic expansion. Perhaps optimism alone might carry us through; but in light of the looming problems facing our integrated world economy, the odds of a sooner-rather-than-later plunge have shortened considerably.

Even as I write, the controversy rages; and about 14 percent of those asked say they are very concerned about Y2K. Of course, another 25 percent or so are not concerned at all. And the other 60 percent just don't care.[2]

Y2K is not the second coming of Christ; yet, neither is it unimportant. It is a real problem that is consuming hundreds of billions of dollars in remedial corrections, and it is very possible that it will consume companies worldwide as supply and transportation systems experience interruptions throughout the year 2000.

It is also possible that the Y2K problem will trigger the largest economic crisis the baby boom generation has ever experienced. Once again, let me repeat that this is my opinion, based on the data I read. I don't claim to be a prophet; I'm just an economist with an opinion.

That said, let me give a few more opinions about the future. Most businesses worldwide have adopted an inventory control system known as "just in time" inventory control. This means they maintain the minimum possible inventory on site and rely on coordinated inventory management systems and reliable delivery systems to get their supplies to them "just in time." Most companies that have adopted this system have reduced their available warehouse space and cannot store additional inventory.

To function properly, just-in-time inventory requires nearly perfect worldwide coordination. That is highly unlikely, with the disruptions Y2K is likely to produce.

I believe that, due to supply and inventory systems interruptions, the Y2K problem will cripple tens of thousands of small and medium-sized companies.

Although the hardest hit businesses will be in noncompliant countries like China, Indonesia, Micronesia, and India, American businesses also will be affected by what happens. In the U.S., where major companies have basically fixed their computer bugs, the economic impact of Y2K will still affect them.

Why? Because we are an integrated worldwide economic system. Virtually no major industry can operate without goods and materials from other countries. Battery manufacturers, for instance, get lead from China, plastics from Indonesia, acid from the U.S., and labor from Mexico. Multiply that by a thousand and you can see what it takes just to build batteries! Even if all of the U.S. were totally Y2K compliant, which it is not, we still could not escape the economic effects of our interdependence with other countries whose businesses are not compliant.

Many large companies that can afford to lease additional warehouse space will increase their available parts inventories in preparation for some Y2K-related disruptions. That will cause an economic uptick in 1999 but a dip in early 2000, as these inventories are drawn down. However, if supply problems persist beyond a month or more, even the large companies will have to slow, or even stop, production.

Smaller companies without the financial resources to ride out the "storm" likely will fail. And, remember, companies of 500 employees or less provide 70 percent of the jobs in the U.S.

Even Europe, our largest trading partner, lags behind the U.S. in Y2K preparedness, as a result of their Euro currency conversions. In fact, the Euro conversion went so well it has given some governments a false sense of security. I heard the representatives of several European countries say, "If we handled a transfer as complex as the Euro with little disruption, Y2K will not be a problem."

Unfortunately, that may not be accurate. European nations spent billions on the Euro, as well as dedicating adequate staff and time. The same cannot be said of their Y2K efforts. One thing about it: When 2000 arrives, we'll know for sure!

The practical truth is that most other countries did not take the Y2K problem seriously enough, soon enough. They are now applying people to the problem, but time is not on their side. By the way, few if any industrialized countries will admit to not being ready by January 1, 2000. It's interesting to me that other countries have caught up with the U.S. in a fraction of the time it took us. From a practical sense, some countries like Mexico, Brazil, and Indonesia lack the financial resources to remedy the problems.

Worldwide, the lack of preparedness or attention given to computer-generated failures likely will cause the problems to last longer and be more severe. Personally, I do not plan to travel to Europe or Asia during the millennium changeover. Air traffic control problems should be a major concern for international travelers.

Why am I so skeptical? For one thing, the White House, which has not been especially forthcoming on the Y2K problem, is starting to get nervous. President Clinton's top Year 2000 specialist, John Koskinen, said that one of his greatest international fears is ensuring the safe operation of 65 nuclear plants located in economically troubled countries. Moreover, the White House warns that failures in electrical, transportation, and telecommunications networks in some foreign countries are all but certain and that these problems are sure to impact the world economy.[3]

Also, I don't buy the "fix-on-failure" solution being trumpeted by those who would have us believe that Y2K will be nothing more than "a bump in the road." According to the fix-on-failure theory, it is a lot cheaper to fix a problem *after* it occurs than before it happens, since it would not require the testing of every system component. Thus, the argument is that the billions of dollars being spent to prevent computer breakdowns could be saved through simple patience. It is the same mindset that believes it is better to put an ambulance at the bottom of a cliff rather than a guardrail at the top.

To better understand fix-on-failure remediation, allow me to use an illustration. If you had a string of 150,000 Christmas lights you wanted to use, and you knew that 100 bulbs had probably failed since the lights were last used, would it make more sense to test all 150,000 bulbs or simply to plug in the strand and replace any that didn't light?

This theory, although sound in principle, is subject to failure when stacked against the hard reality of factors like the shortage of available spare parts and the criticality of the system. As long as you have access to 100 spare lightbulbs, and you don't really need the lights to see, then waiting to correct the defects until the strand is plugged in makes good sense. But what happens if you don't have the spare parts? Or, what if that light string was necessary to keep your father's breathing machine going? You'd end up doing CPR with one hand, while swapping out bulbs with the other.

What if failures are in the computer-controlled train switches and a single failure can create a disaster? Or, what if the Y2K glitch occurs in a Tokyo bank while an electronic funds transfer is being made to a U.S. bank? Instead of a $12 billion transfer being received, it could be erased, ignored, or recorded as $6 trillion. Who really knows for sure?

"Fix on failure" sounds clever and concise, until the failure is in a control circuit in a Russian nuclear reactor that melts down and contaminates half of Europe with radioactive fallout. Or, what if the failure is in the air traffic control computer (or power grid) in the Hong Kong airport, with 50 or 100 jumbo jets approaching? The truth of the matter is that virtually no countries have stockpiled the parts and supplies, not to mention the labor, they will need to fix the failures that occur. And, to make matters worse, there is not enough time left to manufacture and deliver the replacement parts, even if they went on a crash schedule!

Scenarios like these, along with the potential for communication, transportation, and cash flow problems, are part of what prompted The Gartner Group, the leading Y2K consulting company, to predict that more than 20 countries will experience serious failure (interruptions). They also write, "Year 2000 business interruptions will contribute to an economic impact."[4]

A Case Study

Whether individual companies can survive the physical disruptions of Y2K, as well as the longer-term economic impact, will depend on specific factors, such as their size, available cash, and overall preparedness.

Case in point: I have a friend who is a project manager for Y2K for one of the big three car companies. He showed me a chart the company had constructed to assess the Y2K preparedness of 41 countries in which they do business. Specifically, his people looked at each country with an eye toward the things that directly affected their business: transportation systems, communications networks, power grids, and the like. In order for a country to be reflected on the chart, the evidence had to indicate that by the year 2000 the country would be at least 50 to 60 percent compliant (or ready) for Y2K. In other words, there was a 50/50 chance that several critical systems would fail.

As of December 1998, only three countries—the United States, the United Kingdom, and Australia—made the chart. It was calculated that the U.S. will be about 85 percent compliant; the United Kingdom will be about 60 to 75 percent ready; and Australia will be about 65 percent prepared when the clock strikes midnight on December 31, 1999.

The rest of the countries they evaluated—Japan, France, Germany, Italy, Austria, and all our other European allies—were not estimated to be even *5 percent* ready to meet Y2K in their critical systems. Instead of working to find and fix the bugs in their computer systems, these countries have apparently adopted the fix-on-failure solution I described earlier. Without a doubt, most other countries are now working on Y2K compliance.

Some of the most aggressive will likely upgrade their critical systems but few, if any, have the time or money to upgrade all systems. My friend said the cavalier way Japan and much of Asia are treating Y2K makes him wonder if they will ship anything during the first three months of 2000.

You will have to decide if they will be ready or not. Personally, I think not. Check it out for yourself on our Web site: *www.cfcministry.org* or the Gartner site: *www.gartner.com/y2k*.

Y2K: Economic Fallout from the Big Computer Bug

Since the last update of my friend's list, six more countries have been added to the list. However, none, including the U.S., are projected to be 100 percent compliant. The truth is that no one can really be certain of compliance until a totally integrated systems test is run. That test will take place on January 1, 2000—and not before.

What kind of an effect will this global lack of readiness have? Only time will tell. My friend's company, along with many other giant corporations, is girding itself for a battle. According to his analysis, 15 to 20 percent of their small suppliers (500 employees or less) probably will not survive Y2K.

To ensure that his company is not a casualty also, his corporate leaders have gone on the offensive: They have already funneled more than $700 billion into making themselves and many of their key suppliers compliant, and they are increasing their parts inventories by one full quarter by the end of 1999. In addition, to guarantee that the problems will be fixed, the company has actually purchased a number of ill-prepared companies that are necessary to their businesses. When Y2K hits, they will be ready. Or, as he is prone to say, "If anyone is buying cars, we'll be selling them."

Of course, there may not be many buyers, at least in the short term, for the cars his company manufactures. Over a period of time, however, the company expects to reap the benefits of its size and foresight. Like other large, cash-strong corporations, this behemoth likely will have the opportunity to buy not only its suppliers but also some of its competitors in other countries, where the business failures are projected to be even higher than here in the U.S.

Who Stands to Lose from Y2K?

Of course, for every company that may ultimately profit from Y2K, there are plenty of others that will experience only the negative side of this problem. This will be either because they didn't believe the problem was real or because they simply lacked the resources, in terms of money, people, and time, to change their situation. Also, there are companies that will fail—not directly because of Y2K-related problems but simply because the overall economy dips.

Will the "bubble" finally burst and reality set in for the stock market? With all prophetic inferences set aside, I have to believe so, based totally on the economic realities of an eight-year growth cycle, a hyperinflated technology market, and Y2K staring us in the face. At the very least, prudence seems to demand that investors temporarily withdraw from the market until some time around mid-2000.

Dr. Ed Yardeni, chief economist for Deutsche Bank Securities, believes there is a significant chance of a worldwide recession as a direct result of Y2K. He currently estimates the probability of a disruption/recession similar in magnitude to the gasoline shortages that occurred during the Arab oil crisis of the early 1970s.[5]

Other noted financial experts believe the bubble is about to pop, regardless of the Y2K problem. Billionaire George Soros said, "Global capitalism, which has been responsible for the remarkable prosperity of the U.S. in this decade is coming apart at the seams."[6]

I could quote a half dozen other well-respected analysts who believe the economy is poised for an overdue adjustment—down. You will have to decide what path to follow as this story develops.

Those who have invested in highly inflated U.S. companies won't be the only losers in the wake of Y2K or if the "bubble" pops. As the economic fallout spreads over the globe, our trading partners in less-ready-for-Y2K places like Asia and Indonesia will find themselves in an even more precarious financial position. Even after the disasters of the last couple of years, Asia and Indonesia still account for 20 percent of our foreign exports. If these exports were to decline by another half, the result for U.S. companies would be nothing short of an economic disaster.

Y2K: Economic Fallout from the Big Computer Bug

On the political level, public panic or our collective unwillingness as private citizens to deal with the inconvenience and disruptions associated with Y2K could translate into a bigger and more powerful U.S. government. Most Americans live close to the edge financially, and any reduction in their incomes could send taxpayers clamoring for the politicians to "fix" the problems.

Heaven help us if it comes to that. We already see enough evidence of what happens when we rely on government to solve our problems. All too often bureaucrats are prone to smash a gnat with a sledgehammer. Extensive and invasive federal laws and regulations are usually the result of hysteria, on the parts of both citizens and government. Long after the crisis has passed, the laws continue to strip away our freedoms.

The social and moral mess we're in today is, in large part, an outgrowth of Franklin Roosevelt's attempt to "fix" the Depression through government programs, which led to more federal involvement in every area of our lives, from education to crime punishment. As a result, we have crime in our schools, since ethics and morality were systematically eliminated from the classrooms under the guise of "separation of church and state." We have flooded the nation with filth, sex, and violence under the banner of "freedom of speech" (except for religious speech), and we have allowed the slaughter of 30 million unborn children under the banner of "freedom of choice."

You know, as I think about it, I question why God's judgment has not fallen on this nation already. I don't know about you, but I would gladly suffer any calamity if it would bring this nation back to God!

A Christian Response to Y2K

During the past year, I have addressed Y2K on our radio programs, as well as in person, as I spoke to audiences all over the country. Almost everyone I talked with had the same two questions: "How should I prepare for Y2K?" and "What should I do with my money?"

I've already told you what I think will happen; although, as I said earlier, I can't offer any definitive proof that my observations (*not* predictions) will come true. Only time will tell. As to what each of you can do, consider the wisdom of this proverb: *"The prudent sees the evil and hides himself, but the naive go on, and are punished for it"* (Proverbs 22:3). With this verse in mind, I want to offer a four-point strategy for dealing with Y2K that involves **adopting perspective, planning, preparing,** and **providing.**

1. Adopting the right perspective. The short-term effects of Y2K, both in terms of physical disruptions and economic aftershocks, will be alarming. If we could think only six months into the future, the potential for crisis (and panic) is great. But if we extend our time horizon out a year or two, things begin to look a lot more manageable.

Our economy may take a big hit as a result of Y2K, but it will recover, and we will emerge stronger than ever, thanks to the new jobs and technology (specifically the Internet) that will drive our return to financial health. Economic uncertainty is not a new phenomenon. Do not let the specter of Y2K, or any other financial possibility, leave you paralyzed by fear.

If you're planning to start a new business, don't let Y2K keep you from pressing toward your goal, except temporarily. If you want to buy or sell a home, don't let Y2K dictate the timing of your move, unless you think Y2K will bring better deals. As God's Word says, *"Do not boast about tomorrow, for you do not know what a day may bring forth"* (Proverbs 27:1).

No one knows what the future will bring. Instead of trying to run and hide, which is really the bottom line of much Y2K-driven alarmism, recognize that market cycles are inevitable and that the best decisions are typically made within a big-picture, long-term framework.

2. Planning. Operating with a written plan is one of the most effective ways to fight the temptation to think short-term. When you have a well-crafted financial strategy, you can remove yourself emotionally from market swings and other fear-inducing circumstances. A sound financial plan demands an accurate assessment of factors, such as your tolerance for risk, your individual goals, and your age. For example, a 68-year-old man who depends on the income generated by his investments would take a different approach to Y2K than his 34-year-old son, whose children won't need money for college for 15 years.

The market crash of 1929 illustrates the value in having a financial plan—and using it. With a few notable exceptions, such as Bernard Baruch and Joseph P. Kennedy, who read the signs correctly and withdrew their assets from the market, most American investors took a significant economic hit. The vast majority who had borrowed to invest were wiped out.

Even for the two years following the 1929 crash, there were several opportunities to get out with lesser losses, but something (greed, pride, optimism) caused most to ride the downturn all the way to the bottom.

After the final gasp in 1931, investors bailed out of the market in droves (and many literally bailed out, leaping to their deaths from office windows when they concluded that their fortunes really were gone). If these people had been able to stay the course, many would have recovered by 1954—just 15 years later. Then they would have reaped the benefits of continued growth in the market (although the market recovered, not all the original stocks recovered).

Of course, staying the course and sticking with your financial strategy can take a fair amount of nerve, especially when the going gets tough. Knowing how much nerve you have is part of understanding your tolerance for risk, which we will cover later. We'll also look at some age- and personality-appropriate investment strategies in a future chapter. For now, though, I simply want to stress the importance of being proactive, rather than reactive, when thinking about Y2K.

3. Preparing. Although this book is not intended to serve as a survivalist's guide for Y2K, simple prudence dictates that we take some steps to prepare ourselves for the potentially chaotic (or merely inconvenient) days ahead. Volumes of information on physical preparations for Y2K—from tips on storing food to administering first aid—are available through your local bookstore or on the Internet. Rather than repeat that information here, I want to offer a "bare basics" guide to getting ready for the new year.

Financially, you should do all that you can to get out of debt. If a recession hits and you lose your job or find your salary cut, how much debt you have and how well you can control your spending could make the difference in your family's economic well-being. If you need more information or advice for conquering debt, please visit our Web site at *www.cfcministry.org*. Christian Financial Concepts has trained financial counselors throughout the country who specialize in helping people regain their financial footing and manage their money effectively. Someone will reply to your e-mail.

Next, keep a month's supply of cash in small bills on hand as the new year approaches. If you don't need it, you can always put it back in the bank. But if your bank is deluged by panic-stricken depositors, you'll be glad to have some ready cash, especially since communications-sensitive credit cards may not work consistently for the first few days (or weeks) of the new millennium.

And don't wait too long to get your money out; if enough people have the same idea late in 1999, the available supply of currency could be depleted. The Treasury is making additional cash available, which should avert any shortage, but nobody knows how people will react. Besides, your bank requires available power and phone lines to process your orders, just like any other business. Y2K-related computer glitches could make it difficult for you to access your funds after December 31, 1999.

If you decide to take your investment money (in part or in

total) out of the stock market in the last quarter of 1999 (and again, that decision depends on things like your age and temperament), consider parking it in a three- to six-month CD. Gold and other precious metals have not held their value in recent years; and, Treasury bills (also traditionally seen as a secure investment) are fairly illiquid investments, because you usually need to hold them for a year or more. If you have more than $100,000 to invest, you need to work with several banks to be certain your funds are insured by the FDIC.

Obtain copies of important documents, such as your family's birth certificates and marriage licenses. Keep bank and credit card statements, tax returns, investment records, Social Security information, and other financial records in a safe place so you can access them if you need to reconstruct a paper trail in the future.

Concerning supplies, keep on hand about a one-month's supply of nonperishable food and 20 gallons of bottled water per family member. I recommend water that is filtered and ozonated to ensure purity. If the water goes off and you can't take a shower, that's a nuisance. If you have nothing to drink, however, the problem could become serious. For prudence's sake, buy food that you will use eventually, regardless of what happens with Y2K. If the disruptions are minor, you can simply eat the food in the normal course of daily life.

Also consider how you will heat or light your home and how you plan to cook, if and when the power and/or gas is disrupted. Many people have bought generators. For most families this is an unnecessary expense. A more reasonable expense may be to purchase some oil lamps and a two-burner cook stove (keep in mind whether fumes need to be directed outside to avoid carbon monoxide poisoning). If there are no major interruptions as a result of Y2K, you can use them during the next winter ice storm.

4. Providing. For Christians who want to show God's love to a hurting world, it is not enough to simply hunker down and take care of their own families. Jesus commands us, *"Give to him who asks of* *you, and do not turn away from him who wants to borrow from you"* (Matthew 5:42). The apostle Paul echoes this challenge: *"So then, while we have opportunity, let us do good to all men, and especially to those who are of the household of the faith"* (Galatians 6:10).

Y2K is an opportunity. God is neither worried nor surprised by the prospect of a computer-generated technology breakdown, and neither should we be. In fact, it is in difficult times that the Lord often gives His people an even greater platform from which to demonstrate the wisdom of His Word. The specter of Y2K offers believers a chance to show the world that our trust is in God (Who is all-powerful) and to reach people with the message that true security and salvation are found only in Jesus Christ. Prepare to feed and care for your family, and then be alert to the practical needs of those around you.

Again, Y2K represents a unique opportunity, and it's one that we may not have for very long. In the coming chapter we'll look at the assets that characterize our current economy. Many of these factors, such as investor confidence, will almost certainly be shaken when the downturn comes. As our economy begins to recover, as it ultimately will, the confidence will return, along with a hardness of heart where the Gospel is concerned. Don't miss your chance. Adopt the right perspective, plan, prepare, and provide for Y2K.

Then be ready to **proclaim** the good news to a listening world.

Y2K: An Economic View

Before I close this chapter, I will restate what I believe the impact of Y2K on America will be. Much has been said and written about the physical impact of Y2K in terms of potential electrical outages, food shortages, bank closures, and the like. These may well be a reality in other parts of the world, because other countries have not taken this problem seriously, or they simply lack the resources to correct the problems. It *could* happen in the

U.S. as well. I say could because no one *really* knows the true impact of Y2K; it's impossible to test all the changes and fixes until January 1, 2000. But come January 1 (or sooner), Y2K *will be a reality;* then we'll all know the full impact.

As a matter of note here, the Gartner Group estimates that only 8 percent of Y2K-related failures will occur within two weeks of January 1, 2000. Ninety-two percent will occur subsequent to that time through 2000 and 2001.[7]

Personally, I don't expect long-term shutdowns in basic utilities—unless people panic. However, I do expect that we will experience isolated and frustrating outages and shortages—perhaps for several weeks or maybe months.

On the economic level, I believe it is possible that we will see a downturn as thousands of small and medium-sized businesses stumble over Y2K-related problems. Many businesses will fail because they lack the resources to ride out the problems created by inventory shortages from suppliers outside the U.S.

Other basic commodities, such as oil, gas, fresh fruits and vegetables, and currency transfers will likely be compromised when countries that have adopted a fix-on-failure mode find themselves in one crisis after another. The economic impact of this disruption is both unknown and incalculable at this time.

One of the most knowledgeable Y2K experts, Dr. Edward Yardeni of Deutsche Bank Securities (mentioned previously), had been downgrading his estimate of a worldwide recession from 70 percent in June 1998 to 40 percent by June 1999. More recently, though, on his Web site, *www.Yardeni.com,* he upgraded his estimate to 70 percent again as accurate data on the preparedness of government agencies worldwide has begun to surface.[8] It seems that the U.S. and other governments have been exaggerating their readiness. Imagine that!

Those who financially (or emotionally) cannot ride out a recession that may last a few months should take steps to secure their assets.

For most, this may mean selling appreciated stocks, paying the capital gains taxes, and parking the investment funds in CDs or money market accounts. The risk you run if you do that and nothing happens (not likely, but possible) is that you'll miss some potential profits and pay some taxes. The risk you run if you ignore the impact of Y2K is that your assets could take a nosedive (financially speaking), from which it may take years to recover.

The opinions are mine. The decisions are yours.

———————

1. Senator Robert F. Bennett's Senate Special Committee on the Year 2000 Technology Problem, *Investigating the Impact of the Year 2000 Problem: Summary of the Committee's Work in the 105th Congress,* February 24, 1999; Congressman Steven Horn's House Subcommittee on Government Management, Information and Technology, *The Year 2000 Problem: Status Report on Federal, State, Local, and Foreign Governments,* January 20, 1999.
2. "Y2K Not a Major Worry," *USA Today,* May 17, 1999.
3. Associated Press (Washington), "Effects of Year 2000 bug overseas causes worries," *Winston-Salem Journal,* April 22, 1999, A3.
4. Gartner Group, "US personal advice for the Year 2000 problem," January 1999.
5. "Y2K Reporter," *DMG Portfolio Strategy Service,* March 16, 1998. Dr. Yardeni has also published the book *Year 2000 Recession? Prepare for the Worst, Hope for the Best.* " His Web site is *www.yardeni.com.*
6. *The Crisis of Global Capitalism* (Perseus Books, 1998).
7. Gartner Group Web site: *www.gartner.com/y2k* in May 1999.
8. "Y2K Reporter," *DMG Portfolio Strategy Service,* March 16, 1998.

5

The Glass Half Full:
The Good News for Our Economy

Sam looked at me and shook his head, oblivious to the near-perfect putt he had just made. "Internet stocks!" he said incredulously. "You bought Internet stocks? I thought you steered clear of that high-risk stuff."

"Well, normally I do," I admitted, "but you'd have to be half-blind or crazy not to see what's happening; it's a golden opportunity! Internet stocks are virtually a sure thing these days. I've been making 30 to 40 percent returns. Where else are you going to earn that kind of money?"

"Still . . ." Sam said, still questioning based on his own convictions. "It sounds pretty risky the way stock prices jump around. That's not like you."

Sam and I had been good friends for years, and I had a fairly accurate idea of how his investment portfolio was structured. "What kind of returns are you getting?" I asked, baiting the trap.

I could almost see Sam squirm as he struggled with how to couch his answer. Finally he said almost apologetically: "Ten to 12 percent."

"Twelve percent!" I scoffed. "In *this* economy? Well, to each his own, I guess, but let me tell you, you're missing out on the chance of a lifetime, Brother."

Shaking his head, Sam fingered his putter and sauntered over to where his ball lay just outside the cup. He tapped it—much too hard—and then watched helplessly as the ball skirted the hole and rolled to a stop 10 feet on the other side.

The next day I was sitting in my office when the phone rang. It was Roger, our mutual friend and Sam's professional financial advisor. "Sam wants me to get him into Internet stocks," he told me. "He says you told him they were a good deal."

I could hear the accusation in his voice, and I couldn't stifle my laughter. "Don't you do it!" I said. "Sam has always been a conservative, blue-chip investor; he has no business buying that stuff."

"Didn't you buy it?" Roger challenged.

"Absolutely not—at least not anything but Microsoft and a couple of other industry leaders. You know me, Roger. I invest in quality, not hype! I was just pulling Sam's leg. I wanted to see what it would take to get him to switch his investment strategy."

Later that day I got a call from an embarrassed Sam, and we laughed about how well my ruse had worked.

"Why did you do it?" I wanted to know. "What made you decide to change the strategy that has worked so well for you all these years?"

"I guess I just got greedy," Sam admitted. "I couldn't stand the thought of you and everyone else making 30 percent when I was earning a third of that."

Sam was an ideal candidate for my experiment. First, he's a good friend and accepts my eccentricities. Second, he is nearly 70—a retired professional who has done well financially. And, third, he is highly conservative and would not (and should not) normally take excessive risks with his retirement savings.

I knew, though, if I could persuade Sam to change his investment strategy and get into high-risk stocks, anyone is susceptible. That's how frenzies feed frenzies.

Up for Grabs

Sam's motivation to take unrealistic risks with his hard-earned money, embarrassed as he was to own up to it, is actually one of the pillars of our current economy. In an era when casual conversations are dominated more by names like Amazon and eBay than they are by Yankees and Braves, stock market investing has become the new national pastime. Word is spreading on the golf course, at the water cooler, and around the dining room table of 20, 30, and 40 percent returns *per month*!

More money is being pumped into the market than ever before. Approximately 61 percent of Americans have a stake in the market through 401(k) plans and low-cost brokerage accounts; and most of these investors assume that stocks always go up.[1]

This parallels so closely the attitudes of Americans of the 1920s era that it's spooky. Back then stock market investing was a national craze. Ordinary people were quitting their jobs to make their fortunes in the market. Two dangerous attitudes prevailed during the late '20s: one, that it was foolish to *work* for a living when money could be made so easily; two, the market *had* to go up. Much like today, sharp declines in stock prices were viewed as "opportunities" to invest at lower prices. Today we are seeing price swings in the 3 to 5 percent range on a weekly basis.

In this frenetic climate, even a drop of 15 or 20 percent probably would not deter most investors. With so much cash in the market, any dip short of a major crash would likely see speculators coming back in droves, spurred on by money managers who, as one of my stockbroker friends put it, "don't get paid for managing cash." Trading is what earns the fees and commissions and, regardless of how foolhardy they might secretly think their actions are, the money managers will continue to shovel cash into the market as fast as their clients give it to them. For today's money managers to allow a client to sit on the sidelines or to invest strictly in conservative stocks is to invite that client to look elsewhere for financial advice.

I have a friend (we'll call him Harry) whose investment company manages a large amount of money, mostly from Christian investors. I have watched his firm with great interest over the last three years or so. The average rate of return has been between 4 and 6 percent.

Often one of Harry's clients will reflect on his or her company's meager returns and ask what I think. The implication is whether the money should be moved elsewhere to get a greater return. My question is always the same: "Why did you choose this firm in the first place?"

Usually the person will respond, "Because of Harry's integrity and expertise."

"If you had taken great risks and the market had dropped and you had lost a fourth or half of your assets, what would you have said?" I ask. At that point the light goes on with virtually everyone. Obviously, looking back, anyone should have shifted all of his or her assets into the "highfliers." But looking forward, nobody really knows.

For a baby boom generation that has never seen a *real* market downturn since 1987, let alone a recession, it is all too easy to see a drop in stock prices as nothing more than a buying opportunity. And the boomers have no shortage of money to invest. In addition to the paychecks they've earned in a decade of nearly perfect economic conditions, they stand to inherit some $3 to $4 *trillion* from their parents and grandparents in what will be the largest transfer of wealth in history.

Being diligent savers, the postwar generation has spent a lifetime accumulating assets to the tune of about $12 trillion. This is wealth that, over the next couple of decades, will make its way into the coffers of charities, nonprofits, the IRS, and a host of bullish heirs whose philosophy is summed up on a bumper sticker I saw on I-75 headed to Florida: "He who dies with the most toys wins." What a shock the people with that philosophy will have on Judgment Day.

Money Isn't Everything

While a soaring stock market, flush with billions of dollars in investment capital, takes center stage in the economic show, other financial indicators have given analysts plenty more to be positive about. Inflation, which for years in the '70s and '80s kept politicians and market watchers glum-faced on the Sunday morning talk shows, is now almost nonexistent; and prices on imports from Japan and other countries have pushed the cost of many consumer goods to the lowest levels in years. Truly, this is one of the economic phenomena of our generation. In economics courses, one of the fundamentals taught is how inflation occurs: too much money chasing too few products.

If the money managers (the Federal Reserve and our government) create new money out of thin air (credit), consumers will spend more for the products they want; thus prices go up. In a practical sense, we know that's true. Homes cost more now because the use of credit opened the market to more buyers. Imagine the devaluation that would occur in the price of homes if all buyers had to pay cash.

The cost of a college education also has escalated, almost in direct proportion to the ability of parents and students to finance their learning through loans. So why have prices for many consumer products stabilized and even dropped over the last decade? The greater question is, "Has inflation *really* been solved, as some government economists now believe?" All I can tell you about inflation is that unless all the rules of economics have been abolished inflation will return. As long as consumers (citizens and government) spend more than they earn (and they surely do), inflation still lurks around the corner. When? Who knows? But it will return.

At this moment in time we're reaping the benefits of a rapidly accelerating technology that makes our electronic devices faster, more powerful, and cheaper. In addition, with most of the rest of the world in recession or depression, in comparison our currency is stronger than theirs, which makes their products cheaper here. This is the glass "half full." The negative (half empty), as I said earlier, is that our products are more expensive over there, so we export less. So far, the economy doesn't seem to care, but we'll see.

As the following chart shows, we are experiencing severe trade deficits right now. Americans are buying more foreign-made goods than we are selling American-made products to foreign countries. It should be of concern that our outgo exceeds our income. As the saying goes, in such cases our *upkeep* may be our *downfall*.

Record U.S. Trade Deficits

Cheap imports continue to pour into the United States, while our exports are declining to other countries with troubled economies.

This has resulted in the largest monthly trade deficit in our history — the new year began with a $17 billion deficit.

	Imports	Exports
AUG '98	$91.7 Billion	$75.0 Billion
SEP '98	$92.0 Billion	$77.4 Billion
OCT '98	$94.4 Billion	$80.4 Billion
NOV '98	$94.1 Billion	$78.9 Billion
DEC '98	$91.9 Billion	$77.9 Billion
JAN '99	$93.8 Billion	$76.8 Billion

KEY: IMPORTS EXPORTS

Reported in *USA TODAY*
March 19, 1999

Source: U.S. Commerce Department

The Glass Half Full: The Good News for Our Economy

I find it interesting that virtually every day I talk with people who are working two or three jobs and are still falling behind financially. Many workers, especially in the manufacturing sector, have seen their high-paying jobs go to emerging countries where labor is cheap. So there really is a price to be paid for deflation.

Average-income workers have definitely benefited from the economy's overall health, because unemployment for them is virtually nonexistent, as of this moment. Anyone who wants a job today can get one. Moreover, the economic ills that have devastated most of the rest of the globe have left the U.S. standing as the world's only remaining economic superpower.

In fact, it is just such positive indicators that have spurred a whole rash of books and magazine articles championing the belief that our economic boom will never stop. It is an interesting phenomenon that during economic hard times doom-and-gloom books sell well; and during good times prosperity books sell well. I guess people want to think that whatever they have adjusted to won't change. But it will! The very economic factors that make a boom possible plant the seeds of the next recession.

Because of supply and demand, overproduction leads to lower prices for goods, which leads to lower profits for companies, which leads to labor cost reductions (layoffs). This is not a mystical cycle. It is economic reality at work. In every cycle, up or down, there are "experts" who believe that if it's down, it will stay down, or if it's up, it will stay up.

"The rules have changed," the experts assure us. "We are in a new paradigm; old ways of controlling the economy were flawed. We have new models, better laws, and innovative computer programs to promote long-term investing and enhance our prosperity. And, the financial planners say, the investors of today are smarter: We're all in this together, we're more levelheaded than our parents were, and our enthusiasm is well-founded."

Sounds like something out of a 1929 *New York Times* newspaper, doesn't it? I just pray that the optimists are correct, just as I pray that the pessimists are wrong. For now, I'll remain a realist and believe, as the old saying goes, "What goes up must come down."

The following are headlines for the days immediately following the market crash.

The New York Times.

Copyright, 1929, by The New York Times Company.

WORST STOCK CRASH STEMMED BY BANKS; 12,894,650-SHARE DAY SWAMPS MARKET; LEADERS CONFER, FIND CONDITIONS SOUND

Wall Street Optimistic After Stormy Day;
Clerical Work May Force Holiday Tomorrow

(Friday, October 25, 1929)

STOCKS GAIN AS MARKET IS STEADIED; BANKERS PLEDGE CONTINUED SUPPORT; HOOVER SAYS BUSINESS BASIS IS SOUND

TRADING IS NEAR NORMAL

General Electric and Westinghouse Join R.C.A.-Victor Corporation Radio Merger

(Saturday, October 26, 1929)

STOCK PRICES SLUMP $14,000,000,000 IN NATION-WIDE STAMPEDE TO UNLOAD; BANKERS TO SUPPORT MARKET TODAY

Financiers at Meeting Agree Prices Are Now Attractive and Money is Plentiful

(Tuesday, October 29, 1929)

STOCKS COLLAPSE IN 16,410,030-SHARE DAY, BUT RALLY AT CLOSE CHEERS BROOKERS; BANKERS OPTIMISTIC, TO CONTINUE AID

CLOSING RALLY VIGOROUS
INVESTMENT TRUSTS BUY

Bankers Believe Liquidation Now Has Run Its Course and Advise Purchases.

(Wednesday, October 30, 1929)

Technology: The New Revolution

Even if you believe the optimists who are touting a new economic theory, some things truly *have* changed the face of modern investing. Thanks, at least in part, to new tax laws, 31 million Americans (an increase of 48 percent in less than a decade) keep stocks in tax-deferred retirement accounts, which necessitates long-term holding.[2] Other additions, such as the Roth IRA, have made for an investor-friendly environment. And publicly held companies have, in general, reaped the benefits of computer technology and shareholder scrutiny, restructuring themselves to improve efficiency and productivity.

However, the most significant change hasn't come from the government or individual investors but from a technological revolution that, incredible as it sounds, is still in its infancy. We have only just begun to recognize the power of computers and the Internet and the applications that this technology has for every facet of our lives. The Internet revolution that is underway, even as I write, will alter the world as we know it as drastically as television has over the last 50 years—perhaps more.

In his book, *Business @ the Speed of Thought,* Microsoft president Bill Gates describes what is happening to our lives through the Internet in terms of a revolutionary lifestyle. "The adoption of technology for the Web lifestyle is happening faster than the adoption of electricity, cars, TV, and radio. . . . Because the Internet is a worldwide communications infrastructure that depends on electricity, you could say that its popular acceptance is an extension of the 'electric lifestyle.' But the Internet is enabling a new way of life I call 'the Web lifestyle.'. . . The Web will be used to pay your bills, manage your finances, communicate with your doctor, and conduct any business. . . . The adoption of technology for the Web lifestyle is happening faster than the adoption of electricity, cars, TV, and radio."[3]

The following chart helps to show the rapidity with which the computer and the World Wide Web are becoming accepted and used by the general public. I have read that more than 60,000 people go online for the first time every day.

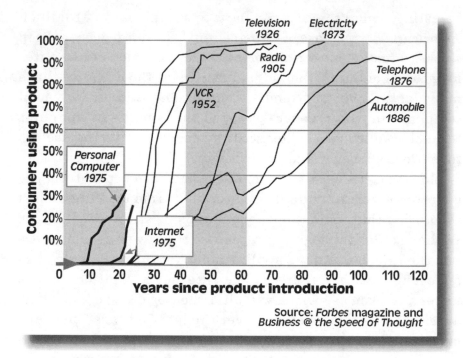

Source: *Forbes* magazine and
Business @ the Speed of Thought

Gates doesn't believe that the growth of the Internet means the death of the established patterns for communicating: speaking face-to-face and writing letters. He doesn't see the new technology depersonalizing; rather, it is an enabler.

It's not surprising that such high value is being placed on everything that is Internet-oriented. Personal computers and the Internet are transforming our world as radically as electricity did in earlier generations.

The fact that millions of people have started home-based businesses is a by-product of this technological revolution. The "virtual" office of the 21st century consists of computers, faxes, modems, cell phones, automated phone attendants, and on and on (what Gates describes as the "digital nervous system"). Home-based employees are lowering the cost of company overhead, shrinking needed office space and all its associated costs (i.e., heat and air, carpets, paint, food service, and so on).

The Glass Half Full: The Good News for Our Economy

At least two people who would otherwise be in-house employees of the Thomas Nelson company (the publisher of this book) worked from their homes via e-mail to help me with this book. This would not have been possible a decade ago but will be the norm in five years. Books (or music, or movies, or whatever) will still be produced but not in the traditional "factory" environment.

Education will change even more drastically (assuming we can work around our government bureaucrats). The university of the future, for example, might not be on a conventional campus where hallowed halls are bordered by brick paths and boxwoods. Instead, education—from kindergarten right on through graduate school—could take place at home or elsewhere: in virtual classrooms, where teachers, lecture notes, and mountains of research and information are accessible through the Internet. Already more than 100,000 college courses are available online, with that number expected to jump to three million within the next two years.[4]

No time to get your bachelor's degree? Don't worry. According to University of North Carolina at Chapel Hill Chancellor Michael Hooker, you may soon be carrying a handheld "knowledge navigator" that can provide instant access to all human knowledge.[5] Whether you want to get stock quotes or learn how to change a flat tire, all the information you need will be yours for the asking.

I have personally benefited from this technological innovation even while compiling information for this book. In the past, the research would have consisted of countless visits to libraries and other data repositories. This time, however, the data was accessed through an Internet-linked PC, using browsers like *Hotbot.com* and *Infoseek.com*. It's like having the *New York Times* archives in my study—unbelievable technology that was only a dream 10 years ago.

The last time we saw a revolution even close to this magnitude was in the years following the Civil War, when an unparalleled outburst of railroad construction united the country and helped touch off the industrial revolution.

The Cotton Gin

It is difficult to say what actually sparked what now is called the American industrial revolution, but I would vote for the invention of the cotton gin, invented by Eli Whitney. Have you ever wondered where cotton comes from? Well, the majority of people today obviously know it comes from plants and always has. But in the 1700s, before Mr. Whitney, the cottonseeds had to be picked out by hand, hence the use of slavery in the southern United States. The work was laborious, backbreaking, and required little training and virtually no education. Hence, slaves fit the bill perfectly, at least in the minds of the cotton growers.

What Mr. Whitney did was change the whole face of the nation and the economics of slavery. He invented the cotton gin and went into business; and the rest, as the saying goes, is history.

Eli Whitney was born in Westborough, Massachusetts. Although he showed no interest in school subjects, he was very interested in mechanical things. He started working with his father's tools and then persuaded his father to allow him to continue working on the farm instead of going to school. At the age of 15 he began making nails in his father's blacksmith's shop and fixing violins for his neighbors.

Whitney became interested in the cotton industry in 1790; and, observing the workers one day picking the seeds out of the cotton fibers by hand, he came to the conclusion that he could build a machine to do that work. He designed and built a machine in 1792 that separated seeds from the fibers of the cotton plant, and with that one invention Whitney virtually single-handedly shut down the slave business in America.

From a practical perspective, he made slavery unprofitable. Machines could simply do the work better and faster, and when the cotton fields lay idle the machines would lay idle as well. It would be another half century before slavery became an issue in America and another decade and a half before the Civil War freed the slaves, but a simple invention changed our society forever.

In my opinion, Eli Whitney started the industrial revolution in America and, in the process, began an economic, social, and political revolution as well.

We can be glad that Eli Whitney was an inventor and not a speculator, because if he had decided to take his cotton gin public and sell shares in "cottongin.com" at exaggerated values, we might still be picking cottonseeds by hand today. But, instead, Whitney sold his machine on the open market to all bidders and began the industrial revolution that continues even today.

The Railroad

The next step in the revolution was laid by the railroad barons of the mid-19th century. For 3,000 years civilization's transportation systems had changed very little, and then along came the steam locomotive and changed the entire world.

Prior to the mid-19th century, the railroad had been relegated to the Eastern Shore of the U.S. Then a few men had the vision to extend the railroad from the East to the West Coast. In spite of seemingly overwhelming odds, the tracks were laid by hundreds of thousands of workers. This began the greatest technological revolution ever to occur, in any country, in any century, in history. It linked the East Coast and West Coast of the U.S. together. The change in technology that our forefathers saw in the 19th century as a result of the railroad was as revolutionary as space travel in our century.

Huge fortunes were made by the railroad barons; but, in truth, bigger fortunes were made as cities sprang up all across the nation, and Americans felt the call to colonize the land between the East Coast and West Coast.

The Lightbulb

This still was not the greatest change of the industrial revolution. Perhaps the greatest change to our lives in all of history was the discovery of electricity by Michael Faraday and the eventual exploitation of that discovery by Thomas Edison. Electricity has done more to change our lives than any other single invention or technological discovery in history.

Thomas Alva Edison was born February 11, 1847. When Edison was 7 years old, the family moved to Port Huron, Michigan, where Edison set up his first chemical laboratory in the cellar of their large home. It's interesting that one of Edison's first jobs was working on a railroad, selling snacks and newspapers. At age 16, Edison took a job as a telegraph operator, and in the following years he got similar jobs on several different railroads.

From the beginning Edison was an avid inventor. One of the first patented inventions was the electric voice recorder. In his search for new telegraphic innovations, he started a service delivering financial news to brokers. As a result of improving the stock ticker in the Golden Stock Telegraph Company, Edison was hired as a superintendent for the company.

At age 24, Edison founded the Western Union Telegraph Company and invented the duplex- and multiplex-telegraph machines; and, interestingly enough, he also invented wax paper. At age 27, Edison invented the electric pen; the mimeograph machine; and then, three years later, he invented a working telephone and a phonograph. He lost out to Alexander Graham Bell in his patent request for the phonograph.

But perhaps the greatest invention of all time was when he, at age 32, successfully completed research on the incandescent lightbulb. Edison had the foresight to see the eventual use of the lightbulb throughout society, even though no homes were wired with electricity at the time. The primary means of lighting a home was either candles, oil lamps, or, if you were particularly affluent, piped-in natural gas.

After nearly 300 failures, Edison discovered a way to make lightbulb filaments last. With his patents in hand, to provide electricity and lights for the populace throughout America, he gathered investors to form the Edison General Electric Company.

Clearly, the invention of the lightbulb and the mass use of electricity have done more to change our world than any other single invention in history, with the possible exception of the invention of the wheel. What would society today be like without the widespread use of electricity? Virtually every convenience and comfort we take for granted today is made possible by electricity. By the way, a single share investment in General Electric from the beginning of the century would make any investor a multimillionaire today.

Later Edison did work on movies and also radio. He was involved with the early experimentation on television as well—all major technological inventions that have helped to shape our society today.

The Factory

Henry Ford, the oldest of six children and the grandson of Irish immigrants, was born in 1863 in Dearborn, Michigan. Although raised to take over the family farm, he also was an avid experimenter. Once, in order to observe the power of steam, he plugged up the spout of his mother's teakettle of boiling water and blew it apart. Ford's father allowed Henry as a boy to tinker with many of the tools on his farm. Neighbors and friends considered him a natural-born mechanic.

Perhaps the most significant next step of the industrial revolution occurred in 1876 when the 13-year-old Henry Ford, while riding with his father in a wagon, saw a steam engine traveling along the road under its own power. He jumped off his father's wagon and questioned the driver about his remarkable engine. The steam engine originally had been used for stationary purposes, such as sawing wood. But the engine had been mounted on wheels and was used to propel the platform from one location to another. The engineer operating the device explained all about the machine and even let young Henry fire up the engine and run it. Later, when Ford was a multimillionaire running a huge automobile conglomerate, he said, "That one event showed me that I was by instinct an engineer."[6]

It's interesting how events go in circles, and God uses those events to accomplish His plans. Ford decided not to work on the farm, moved to the city, and found a job at the Michigan Car Company of Detroit for $1.10 a day. He was fired almost immediately thereafter because he angered the older employees by making repairs on machines in a fraction of the normal time. Ford worked at a variety of odd jobs, but he never gave up his dream of developing the universal horseless carriage.

In an interesting sequence of events, in 1891 Ford took a job with the Detroit Edison Illuminating Company, one of Edison's companies. It was through working there that the young Ford met Edison. After discussing his ideas with the great inventor, Edison told Ford, "Young man, you have a good idea. Keep at it." This single meeting with Edison gave Ford the renewed spirit and encouragement he needed to change the face of a nation in the next step of the industrial revolution.

Ford had produced an operable car by 1899. After several false starts that lost several investors lots of money, on June 16, 1903, with 10 investors, Ford incorporated the Ford Motor Company and set out to manufacture the Ford Model T. A single share in the Ford Motor Company in 1903 would today make any investor a multi-multimillionaire.

But it was not just the design of a workable automobile that helped Ford change our nation. It was the concept of the automated assembly line, where one person did a specialized task on a multitask project. This concept has totally revolutionized the industrialized world as we know it today. Henry Ford did not invent the automobile; he invented the manufacturing technique that allowed mass-produced, low-priced automobiles to be marketed to a general population. You and I drive automobiles that are affordable today because of Henry Ford's innovative genius.

Communications

The last step in the modern industrialization of America was the invention of the wireless and the development of the Radio Corporation of America (RCA). Eli Whitney started the circle with the cotton gin. The railroads made transportation on a mass scale possible. Edison invented the lightbulb and wired the cities with electricity. America was set for a revolution that would change our society and the world forever. A relatively obscure inventor, Marconi, invented a wireless communications device called a radio.

Edison's company, General Electric, bought the U.S. patent rights to the radio and brought it to the United States. General Electric made the radios, but a group of investors formed what is now called RCA, the Radio Corporation of America, to market not only radios but also the use of the radio, which created our current broadcasting system. For the first time, investors recognized the potential to influence society, based on mass communications, and the Radio Corporation of America came into existence to influence the thinking habits of America. Later, radio and television changed the buying habits of Americans, the morality of society, and ultimately society itself.

Just consider what massive changes our world has seen over the last 100 years. We went from horse-drawn carriages to steam locomotives to space travel. We went from gaslights and coal lamps to electric lights and power to operate everything from refrigerators to microwaves. Radio changed our home life, and television changed our values. We have become the product of these inventions over a period of 150 years or less. It's no wonder that we are, in fact, a schizophrenic society that has lost our core value system. And it is quite possible that even greater changes will occur over the next 50 years.

I believe that the invention of the Internet is not simply a better means of connecting computers together, any more than the invention of the radio was a better means of sending a voice over longer distances. The invention of the radio gave us the ability to create intellectual products and then spread them to every home in America. The Internet today is a means to distribute information to literally billions of people simultaneously throughout the world. It's going to change our grandchildren's society more than radio and television have changed ours.

Recently I was at a missionary conference, talking to the information systems manager, and I asked, "How has the Internet changed what you're able to do as a missionary group?"

He said, "It has changed our productivity and our communications more than any other invention in history. We're now able to connect our missionaries, even in the middle of the jungle, on the Internet via a satellite system. On a daily basis, we can transmit and receive information. We have missionaries in the middle of the South American jungles who are doing translations for new tribes. Almost daily their translations are transmitted to our headquarters, where our researchers and interpreters review them, send the results through a word processing program, and return the documents the next day to the missionaries—complete and intact. We're able to provide them with research data that otherwise never would have been available in the jungles."

He added, "On a monthly basis, we're able to bring all of our missionaries to a chat room on the Internet, where we all discuss our common problems and find solutions. Our missionaries now feel linked together. Only five years ago it would have required a trip into the jungles just to talk to our missionaries and would have cost thousands of dollars."

That's the good side of the Internet. Of course, there's a bad side also. We've seen evil grow in our society as a result of the radio and television and, most assuredly, motion pictures. But much of the bad is there because the good wasn't available. Where a light does not exist, the darkness is intense. I believe that's what we're seeing in the media today.

But we should not withdraw from this new technology simply because of the bad. We need to get involved and make it more useful to the good side—God's side. We sit on the threshold of an information revolution. This information revolution will dominate the 21st century. This new revolution is going to create great wealth and great opportunity, and that's the good news. The bad news is that we really aren't any smarter than our ancestors. All of this new technology will not change the rules of economics. Ups and downs will still occur. Some investors will prosper; others will suffer as a result.

In the next chapter we'll be talking about the "half-empty" glass, and perhaps the news that you won't hear from your own broker.

---

1. David Rynecki, "Finally, Dow 10,000," *USA Today*, March 3, 1999, A1.
2. Ibid.
3. Bill Gates, *Business @ the Speed of Thought* (New York: Warner Books, 1999), 115–117.
4. David Rice, "Chancellor Predicts 'Virtual Universities,'" *Winston-Salem Journal*, March 23, 1999, A1.
5. Ibid.
6. Henry Ford Biography, *edison–ford–estate.com/ford*.

6

The Glass Half Empty:
The News You Won't Hear from Your Broker

Many years ago I read a story about the Pony Express. The horses were big and strong and fast. Day or night, summer or winter, daring young unarmed riders leaped into the saddle to ride from Missouri to California—a distance of nearly 2,000 miles. To ride a slow horse or one that tired easily across a desolate prairie was to invite disaster—often in the form of an attack by Indians or bandits.

Fresh horses were stationed every 10 miles or so, saddled and ready to go. Would-be attackers found themselves thwarted when their smaller ponies failed to keep pace with the superior thoroughbreds. Eventually, though, the Indians wised up. Spreading themselves out along the path, they stationed their own fresh mounts every half-mile or so. When the Pony Express rider came along, he could easily outrun the first few Indians. But as new pursuers joined the chase, the gap narrowed. The rider could spur his horse and will it to speed, but there was no getting around the fact that, after about 25 minutes of hard running through the desert, the horse would drop dead. And all the while the Indians kept closing in. Left with no alternatives, except certain death, the Pony Express riders would whip their valiant steeds until they literally fell in their tracks.

In truth, the Pony Express lasted a lot longer in the movies than it ever did in real life. And even though the venture was a financial failure and folded within 18 months, during that time the Pony Express missed only one trip of weekly or biweekly operations, which is truly remarkable considering the conditions of the time.

That image of horses being whipped into exhaustion is a relatively accurate analogy for what is happening in our stock market and economy today. Anybody with any degree of common sense or market savvy knows that 15 or 20 percent per annum returns are not the norm and that the 200 to 300 percent profit per *year* that some investors claim to make is historically impossible to sustain. These phenomenal returns cannot continue forever; and, deep down, reasonable people know it. But every time we turn around we see another Indian, so we just keep on whipping this economy in the backhanded hope, I guess, that somehow this economic cycle will defy all logic and continue indefinitely.

So far we have taken stock of our economic assets—factors such as low unemployment rates, nonexistent inflation, and a stock market that seemingly can do no wrong. But we've also seen some of the liabilities that are currently crouched at our doorstep: our national and personal debt load, the ripening potential for tariff wars in a recession-strapped global market, and the looming specter of Y2K. But these things aren't the only problem areas. In this chapter, we'll look at a few more trouble spots—facts and trends that could become a significant drain on an otherwise robust economy.

Our Cheap Labor Force

Fueled by birth and immigration, the U.S. is shaping up to become one of the largest Hispanic countries in the world—actually we are already the fifth largest. According to some projections of the U.S. Census Bureau, the Hispanic population in our country will grow from 24.1 million in 1992 to more than 80.4 million by the year 2040.[1] Economically, at least initially, this trend will have some very positive consequences, as both small and large U.S. companies benefit from lower labor costs. Longer term, however, the negative impact will likely begin to outweigh the positives.

Unlike second- and third-generation immigrants, these newly arrived aspiring citizens lack adequate education and, just as important, they lack contacts in the U.S. infrastructure.

This topic is not often discussed, but knowing someone on the inside is very important, and it takes generations for these contacts to work their way up the corporate ladder. The recent emergence of an upper- and middle-class black population is an example of this. Once in place, this group can help pull their friends and family up after them, but it does take time.

To be sure, our new Hispanic immigrants bring with them the willingness to work and strong family ties. But without the economic resources, many, if not most, of them will draw more from the system than they will contribute, which will place a heavy economic strain on their communities.

For instance, school systems will need to adjust to bilingual teaching methods. Health clinics and emergency rooms will be forced to absorb the high medical costs of treating millions of uninsured workers and their families. Working at lower wages and without the benefits of company-sponsored pension or retirement plans, the immigrants will not be able to set aside much, if anything, for retirement, which means that 30 or 40 years from now we could have an additional 100 million aging retirees to support.

And in the shorter term, if an economic downturn forces businesses to scale back or shut down their operations, the immigrants will be among the first to lose their jobs. With little education and no work, they will (of necessity) draw *from* the system. It is difficult enough to pull up roots and relocate in a foreign society, but if the economic expansion dries up there is the potential for social unrest.

Medical Care for Aging Boomers

Hispanic immigrants are not the only ones who will need subsidized medical care. As the baby boom generation ages, money spent on health care will increase dramatically. In 1995 Medicare beneficiaries paid an average $2,563 per person out of their own pockets to pay for additional premiums, services, and products that were not covered by the program—almost one-third of their total health care expenses.[2] There is a logical reason why underwriting companies charge so much to insure people over 65: they use a lot of health-care services. And unlike their postwar parents, the boomers are not used to hardship. They will not tolerate inconveniences.

As costly as Social Security is, the staggering potential cost of Medicare outweighs all other social experiments. It seems probable that health care eventually will be socialized to a high degree. We fought back Hillary Clinton's concept of national health care, but the statistics are clear. The only logical way to make a system that is providing health care for the costliest group (older people) solvent is to manage it with the least costly group (younger people) and raise the prices for everyone.

Unless there is a major scientific breakthrough in health care that inhibits the aging process, the next generation of young families will get stuck with our health bills. In truth, living for today (as the baby boom generation does) has a high future cost.

Technology is great and medical technology has given doctors great tools for everything from peering into our bodies without cutting holes to painlessly removing cataracts. But, these innovative machines come at a *high* cost. I should know. At least twice a year I use several imaging systems to keep check on my cancer status. The question is, "How will the taxpayers of 2015 and beyond pay all the bills?" There will be fewer of them and more retirees.

The following chart shows the dwindling number of wage-earning workers who will be called upon to fund Medicare with their tax dollars.

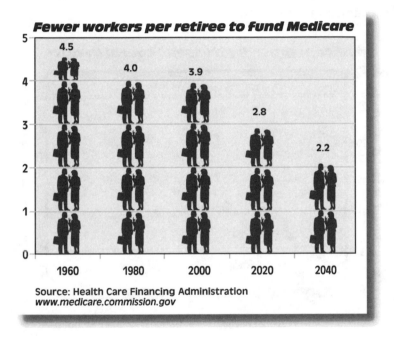

Fewer workers per retiree to fund Medicare

Source: Health Care Financing Administration
www.medicare.commission.gov

You might say, "That's 15 years from now, so why worry about it?" Because the suggested "fixes" require raising taxes (and a lot of them) *right now*! The longer we wait to deal with the future cost, the more difficult and costly it will be. For instance, we could have solved the Social Security problem in the '50s by actually accumulating and investing the surpluses and gradually raising the retirement age. By 2025 the annual deficits will be beyond control. The same will eventually be true of Medicare.

When the first of 77 million baby boomers begin entering the federal Medicare system in the year 2011, annual Medicare expenditures will climb from $207 billion (in 1998) to between $2.2 and $3 trillion in the following 20 years.[3] The stresses that will be caused as senior health care becomes such a large portion of our federal budget may affect the funding of other important programs in national defense, justice, health and safety, and environmental protection.

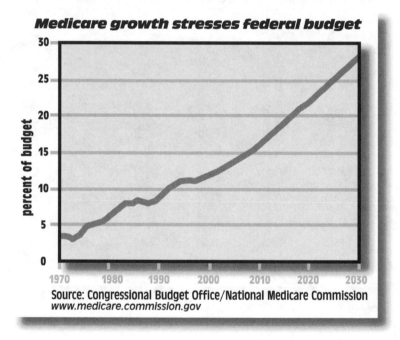

Medicare growth stresses federal budget

percent of budget

Source: Congressional Budget Office/National Medicare Commission
www.medicare.commission.gov

With a relatively small changeover in our Congress, the tax-and-spend advocates could invoke some *big* tax increases and justify them with the same scare tactics we saw used to kill all attempts to reform Social Security in 1994–95. Who cares that the rich generate jobs and already pay more than 80 percent of all taxes? We'll tax them to keep the system alive—and tax our grandchildren too!

China: An Enemy in the Making?

As I noted earlier, as of today, the U.S. is the world's only acknowledged superpower; even so, you can't open a newspaper these days without reading something about China and its rise to prominence. Despite blatant human rights abuses, clear indications of nuclear-weapons spying, and illegal campaign contributions by China, we continue to send massive amounts of money and technology across Chinese borders—money and technology, it would seem, that have the potential to turn China into the world's next great threat.

I believe Lenin said that American capitalists will compete with each other to sell us the rope to hang them. Nowhere is that more evident (in my opinion) than in our China policy. We give them whatever we have and ask little or nothing in return. We export technology that makes their missiles more accurate and reliable, all the while knowing that they will target U.S. cities as a result. Is that nuts or what?

Every week we read of Chinese crackdowns on religious dissidents, mostly Christians, for believing that there is a God. These dissidents are shipped off to prison and used as slave labor to make the very products that Christians in the U.S. then buy. What we saw from Japan during World War II is but a taste of what an Asian war machine of 200 million soldiers is capable of doing. With the added threat of nuclear weapons, this world could be a hostile environment for our children and grandchildren.

The heightened tensions and suspicions between the U.S. and China have another side. What our leaders fail to address, at least publicly, is the incredible cost of rearming ourselves if the diplomatic gloves come off at some future date. Two of the gravest threats to world peace are an aspiring superpower and a widespread economic collapse. Let us never forget that's where Stalin, Hitler, and Mao Tse-tung all got their power. It's also important to remember that it was World War II that solved the

Great Depression in the U.S.—*not* the New Deal. The temptation for nations to go to war is always present. Severe economic problems often provide the motivation to attack one's neighbors. Nuclear missiles make everyone "neighbors."

Moral Bankruptcy

When reports of extramarital affairs and questionable business dealings failed to derail Bill Clinton's presidential bid in 1992, political pundits surmised that, as far as the nation as a whole was concerned, character-related issues no longer mattered. Clinton's 1996 victory, coming despite even worse allegations of presidential wrongdoing, seemed to prove the point. "It's the economy, stupid," became a catchphrase for the Clinton camp. As long as the economy was in good shape, what the president or his aides did on their own time was none of our business.

As a Christian, it is difficult for me to believe that God will continue to bless a nation that denounces Him, as we seem to be doing. From the practical side, there are many consequences of the lack of values in our society. Every day we read about the escalating murder rate among teens—by teens. The increase in AIDS and venereal diseases directly reflects the lack of moral training; and crime in general makes many neighborhoods war zones after dark.

Contracts today are little more than futile exercises in tricky wording that pit one attorney against another—at great expense.

God's patience is long-suffering, but it won't last forever. It is my personal belief that God will punish this or any other nation for its disobedience. Just because it hasn't happened yet doesn't mean that we have escaped God's attention. God warned Israel countless times before He sent the Babylonians to utterly destroy them. Even then He returned them from captivity because He loved them. But also don't forget the recovery was hundreds of years later. I pray we'll be able to repent and seek God's face before He is forced to drive us to our knees.

The Glass Half Empty: The News You Won't Hear from Your Broker

Our valueless society ought to be of grave concern to those who value the economy above all else. When moral character collapses, the economic ramifications can also be devastating. Just ask the 50-plus percent of Americans who have experienced the pain of divorce, most of which was caused by financial problems. In addition to the emotional trauma of a marital breakup, divorce tends to leave both partners—and especially the woman—worse off financially than when they were married.

We now have 11 million single parent families in America. Their average annual income is about $15,000. That is below the government's established poverty level. A *morally* bankrupt society also creates *financial* bankruptcy.

Political decisions can have some financially devastating consequences. The most obvious of these was the Supreme Court's 1973 decision to legalize abortion. Personally I am morally and biblically opposed to the killing of the unborn; however, regardless of where you stand, no one can deny the economic impact of that decision.

In his book, *The Cost of Abortion,* Lawrence F. Roberge says the government published figures on surgical abortions (1.37 million in 1996) do not include mechanical (IUD) and chemical ("morning after" and "birth control" pills) methods, which serve to stop the attachment or development of a fertilized egg. He quotes the estimate of Dr. Bogomir Kuhar (president of Pharmacists for Life) that between 9.6 and 13.4 million abortions occur in the U.S. each year, using all of these methods. In order to maintain our current population, our country requires 2.1 births per woman—because of abortion, we are producing fewer babies than that.[4]

In my book, *What Ever Happened to the American Dream* (Moody Press, 1993), I asked, "What society can absorb the loss of 40 million consumers, not to mention taxpayers, and hope to remain economically viable? Think of the millions of diapers, clothes, toys, and other consumable items that will never be produced or sold. Assuming this lost generation would have had an average annual consumption of $10,000 (a low figure) by 2010, the retirement decade for the baby boomers, the net annual loss to our economy will be at least $400 billion."

For the sake of this discussion, I will ignore the goods and services that more than 30 million aborted Americans would be buying today. Roberge claims abortion has already eliminated a million or more teaching jobs; but let's ignore the jobs created by the demand for schools, food, clothing, houses, and recreation they would have created. Let's just consider the impact on our tax structure.

According to the Tax Foundation, the 1998 local, state, federal, and corporate tax burden was $9,939 for every man, woman, and child in the country. "Social insurance taxes" last year accounted for 28.6 percent of this burden (or $2,847 each). These fund federal entitlements like Social Security, Medicare, and so on. So a rough estimate of the taxes that the more than 30 million aborted taxpayers would have contributed during that year alone is $300 billion—with over $80 billion earmarked for Social Security and Medicare.[5]

In addition to financial loss, we've paid a great societal cost for tolerating abortion. If we carry out family growth projections until the year 2015 (more than 40 years since abortion became legal in our country), we wonder how this generation-that-never-was might have contributed to solutions for many of our economic, health, and social problems. In fact, a recent Internet teen survey revealed that many teenagers wonder if any of the babies destroyed by abortion would have discovered the cure to cancer, AIDS, and other devastating diseases. Talk about shooting yourself in the foot!

Bankruptcy—A Moral Problem

Perhaps the most visible link between a valueless society and economic problems can be seen in our current bankruptcy rate.

The Glass Half Empty: The News You Won't Hear from Your Broker

In years past, bankruptcy was a last-resort option, as people sought to avoid the social and financial stigma that came with legally declaring their insolvency. Today, however, bankruptcy has become an accepted—and in some quarters, even encouraged—means of dealing with debt. In 1997, in the midst of a booming economy, 1.3 million U.S. households filed for bankruptcy—an all-time high.[6]

In 1998 that number was 1.4 million. It is projected that 2.3 million families will file bankruptcy by 2001.[7] You don't have to be a financial genius to recognize the negative impact so many insolvent families can have on the economy.

Since bankruptcies can be recorded on credit reports for up to 10 years, these families are faced with higher financing rates. In addition, lenders automatically build in a price hike to compensate for their losses. Thus, we all pay for bad credit, even if we pay our bills on time.

What Goes Up . . .

Our immigrant population, rising medical costs, national defense, and particularly our nation's moral bankruptcy must all be reckoned as economic liabilities. However, even more than these issues, the current state of our economy could spell trouble all by itself. The overall growth in our technology-driven market has masked a steady erosion in the equity value of many companies that are feeling the effects of the global recession.

A relatively few company stocks have driven the indexes to dizzying heights. As with the "Nifty Fifty" stocks[8] of the '70s that suddenly collapsed, such a narrow-based bull market can turn bearish very quickly. I don't want to rain on anyone's party, but the norm for a bull market (excluding wartime) is about seven years.

The current bull market and economic expansion actually began in the last year of President Bush's administration, which makes it nearly a nine-year growth cycle—the longest peacetime expansion on record. And, not to be capriciously repetitious, but *what goes up must come down.*

Let me rephrase that: Unless we really have changed the fundamentals, what goes up must come down. Clearly, the American public shows a remarkable lack of concern over the future of the record-setting bull market. This overconfidence, coupled with the convenience and accessibility of online trading, has transformed many longer-term investors into day-trading speculators.

Day traders represent the epitome of get-rich-quick in risk-taking. They are, in general, inexperienced investors who trade minute-by-minute in the latest fad stocks. Selection is made based on a stock's movement and virtually nothing else.

"You get the impression that the stock market is kind of fun, not a serious matter at all," says Wall Street's Peter Bernstein, founder of the *Journal of Portfolio Management.* Indeed, according to a recent Gallup/Paine Webber poll, investors *expect* to see returns of 15 percent or more over the next 12 months.[9] But have these optimists checked their history books? Stocks—even those held long term—don't always go up.

Let me illustrate the point. In the March 8, 1999 issue of *Forbes* magazine, David Dreman reveals how "red-hot new issues" have provided horrendous returns on average. He reports, "A study of new issues between 1970 and 1990 showed a median return of minus 45 [percent] over five years. But people ignore the averages while focusing entirely on memorable exceptions."[10]

Since 1900 the Dow has gone down in 24 percent of all five-year periods and 14 percent of 15-year periods. Even 20-year timelines are no guarantee of success.

Economist Robert Shiller of Yale says that, adjusted for inflation, stocks were down for long-term cycles. They dropped by 54 percent in the 20-year period ending in 1919, by 63 percent ending in 1949, and by 29 percent in the 20-year cycle ending in 1986.[11] Shiller points to high price-earnings ratios (PER) as a significant factor in explaining these losses. Price-earnings ratios factor heavily in Wall Street's model for assessing whether stocks are overvalued; and, as this chart shows, today's ratios (from 1974 to 1999) are higher than ever.

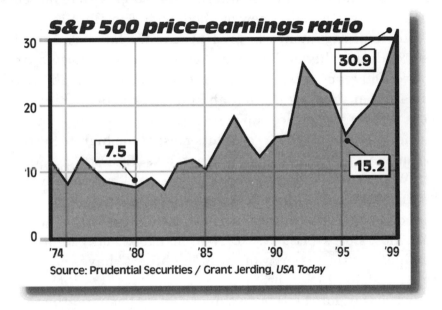

S&P 500 price-earnings ratio

Source: Prudential Securities / Grant Jerding, *USA Today*

Why are these elevated numbers so important? As I mentioned earlier, the price-earnings ratio (PER) is the price you pay for a stock compared to the average annual earnings of the company. For instance, let's say you bought a stock for $100 and the company earns $10 per share per year. That stock would have a PER of 10:1 (10 to 1). (The stock's price, in other words, is equal to 10 times its earnings.)

Now suppose you bought that same stock for $100, but it had earnings of $1 per share. In this case, the stock's price of $100 would be equal to 100 times its earnings (i.e., a PER of 100:1). Ignoring the speculative value of the stock, it would take 100 years of trailing earnings to recoup your initial $100 investment.

Historically, the averages of the S&P stocks on the NY Times Index have ranged between 11:1 and 14:1. As I write this, the price-earnings ratio of the overall market is about 32:1, which is considerably higher, I might point out, than the 1928 precrash average of 22.[12] Some analysts argue that historical ratios are no longer relevant and that the unprecedented growth of our current economy demands a new method for stock valuations.

This same argument was presented in the late '20s as PERs rose to all-time highs. Perhaps they will prove true this time around. Only time will tell. Conventional wisdom, though, would indicate that the Dow is too high and that the only thing that keeps driving stock prices up is "the greater sucker theory."

The NASDAQ market represents most of the high-tech startup companies that are commonly touted as "the future of America." Well, the companies may be, but the stock prices represent the financial equivalent of playing Russian roulette. A very few technology stocks accounted for most of the NASDAQ growth in 1998. Most stocks on the NASDAQ exchange actually went down in value. And the majority of these "highfliers" have yet to generate one dollar in real profits.

By the way, for the Dow to achieve an 18 percent growth for the next 10 years (what a typical young investor now expects), the industrial average would have to reach 42,000 by the year 2009, and 1,000,000 by 2030. If, on the other hand, the Dow returned to its 100-year norm of a 14.3:1 PER, it would result in an average market value of 4,400. That's correct: a Dow of *4,400*!

The only logical way for the Dow stock averages to continue to soar is for company profits to soar also. But, in fact, total gross profits for the Fortune 500 companies declined from 23.2 percent in 1996, to 7.8 percent in 1997, to 4.0 percent in 1998, even while stock prices soared 21 percent in 1996 and 30 percent in 1997. Is this a "bubble" developing or what?[13]

A Generation of Suckers?

According to the "greater sucker theory" (a term coined, I believe, by Dr. John Kenneth Galbraith, legendary economist), if you ignorantly buy a stock for more than it is really worth, you can always sell it to a less knowledgeable buyer at a higher price. Recently a friend in the investment business put it this way: "If you're dumb enough to buy something at more than you know it's worth, there's probably somebody dumber than you out there who'll buy it from you at a higher price—you hope." Under that scenario, a stock's price-earnings ratio becomes almost irrelevant. You don't care about a stock's *earnings*; all that matters is its *trade value*. If the value goes up, you can sell the stock at a profit.

For instance, if you purchased a share of an Internet company's stock today, with a price-earnings ratio of 240:1, it would take *240* years to get your money back (through earnings alone!). Obviously, then, few people are buying such a stock because of its earnings. People buy it because they expect its price to go up; they are looking at its speculative *growth* potential, and the fact that if its value goes up they will be able to sell it for more than they paid.

There are two reasons, then, to buy a particular stock. The first is because of its potential earnings, either currently or in the future. (You might see something to make you believe that earnings will increase in the future, which could make buying the stock a wise financial move.) In this case, you might plan to hold the stock and reap the benefits of its potential earnings. The other reason for buying a stock is because you think its value, or price, will go up. In this case, you would buy the stock with an eye toward selling it in the future. In the current market, day traders often buy stocks and sell them within minutes. This probably is the same mentality that sparked the tulip mania.

Most long-term investors buy stocks with both factors in mind—earnings and growth potential. Usually, they buy the industry leaders, with an eye to future growth (capital gains); but, even if they don't grow spectacularly, they can still expect a return via the dividends distributed from the companies' earnings.

By contrast, many of today's novice investors are jumping in and out of the stock market at a rate not seen since 1928—meaning that the cash being pumped into the market is coming from growth-oriented speculators, rather than from investors who are interested in income from a company's earnings. Many of the younger traders, under the age of 30, as I noted earlier, have never experienced a major market downturn. They expect prices to only rise, and they buy accordingly. It seems we have developed a whole generation of "suckers" (wealthy suckers, to be sure, but what happens when the party is over?).

Currently, more than 38 percent of all household financial assets are in stocks.[14]

If those assets—or even a portion of them—disappear, it's not hard to imagine the shock wave that would be felt in every sector of our society. A prudent observer only needs to look toward Japan, where stocks were assumed to be the key to security, in order to recognize that markets tend to seek their "norms." Does that mean then that we should pull our money out of the market and park it in CDs or Treasury bills, where it will be safe? For some the answer might be yes, at least in the short term.

I believe that there are fortunes to be made for the kingdom of God, provided His people act with wisdom; but blind faith in the market certainly won't do it. Everybody has an opinion, and most of them are usually wrong.

In my opinion, the market is going to return to a more rational norm, motivated by a dose of economic reality. In the next chapter I will share with you the same counsel I have taken myself, what I *think* will happen in the economy over the next several years, and specifically what we can do to prepare for the future.

The Glass Half Empty: The News You Won't Hear from Your Broker

1. *Statistical Record of Hispanic Americas, 2nd Edition*, p. 84; *USA Today*, December 4, 1992, 8A.
2. 1995 Medicare Current Beneficiary Survey, HCFA; *http://medicare.commission.gov*, June 1999.
3. Ibid.
4. Lawrence F. Roberge, *The Cost of Abortion* (Four Winds Publishing). Roberge is a biomedical scientist and biotechnologist consultant who has done research in neuroscience, psychology, and reproductive medicine.
5. Tax Foundation: *www.taxfoundation.org*, June 1999.
6. Nancy Stancill, "Hip-deep in card debt," *Charlotte Observer*, October 18, 1998, 10A.
7. *VISA Risk Management*, 1999.
8. The "Nifty Fifty" stocks of the early 1970s carried an average PE ratio of 40. Some of them, including Philip Morris, Pfizer, Bristol-Myers, Gillette, Coca-Cola, Merck, American Home Products, and Pepsi, outperformed the Standard & Poor's 500 over the next 25 years. However, none of the technology stocks of that time has managed to outperform the index over the same period, including: IBM, Xerox, Digital Equipment, Texas Instruments, Burroughs, Kodak, and Polaroid (*Wall Street Journal*, April 15, 1999).
9. David Henry, "Street Talk: Buffett sees Dow 10,000 as bad news," *USA Today*, March 30, 1999, 3B.
10. "The Contrarion Bubble Psychology," David Dreman, *Forbes*, March 1999.
11. Henry, "Street Talk," *USA Today*, March 30, 1999.
12. Dreman, *Forbes*, March 1999.
13. Nelson D. Schwartz, "A downshift in Profit Growth," 1998 Fortune 500 Introduction, *www.pathfinder.com/fortune/fortune399*, February 11, 1999.
14. John Waggoner, "Feeling the Impact of 10,000 Stunning Stock Action Pervades U.S. Culture," *USA Today*, March 30, 1999, 1B.

7

So, What's Really Going to Happen?

Jerry opened the paper to the business pages and ran a practiced eye over the stock prices. Most of his holdings were up—some only a little, but most were up substantially, he noted with satisfaction. The market had seen some pretty wild swings lately, but Jerry wasn't worried. Only the novice investors panicked when stock prices took a hit. Jerry prided himself in his ability to keep a cool head; the way he saw it, a market downturn represented nothing more than a good opportunity to buy.

Like so many Wall Street watchers, Jerry had heard the gloom-and-doom reports from those who predicted an imminent financial disaster. But they had all been wrong. The market absorbed a 5 percent drop and then rallied. It was clear, at least to him, that a new paradigm had developed: there was so much money pouring into the market and, seemingly, nothing could halt the rise. The doomsdayers were easy to dismiss, especially when you considered how much money was being made. The last major market depression had been, what, 70 years ago? As one of Jerry's colleagues put it, "The country is sound, business is good, and we've got a president who understands how to keep the economy moving. Why should we worry?"

"Why indeed?" Jerry said, as he thought of his brother-in-law. Several months ago, Charles had heard some economist talking about the disastrous drop in U.S. exports, as he called it, and Charles had pulled his money, his life savings, out of the market. As a result, he had missed out on one of the biggest financial gains in history.

Charles was too uptight. He really was a nice guy but too skittish. There were always risks associated with the stock market; Jerry knew that, but that's what made it so much fun. And if Charles had any common sense, he would see that the country's economic problems were easily outweighed by technological advances and industrial developments: signs of progress that promised to propel America to even greater heights. High-tech stocks were making fortunes for him and his friends, and he did not intend to let the bulls pass him by. In just a couple more years he'd be financially independent.

He almost called Charlie again but decided against it. The last time his sister had snapped at him about being too reckless. "Well, to each his own," he sighed as he tried to catch the latest quotes. *Trading is down, but that's normal for the season,* he thought. *Usually there are more sellers than buyers in the months before Christmas. People cash out some stocks to pay bills and to buy gifts for their families.*

By noon the Dow had dropped again. Jerry put in a buy order, which was filled immediately. An hour later the Dow was down sharply. Jerry stopped buying and numbly watched as the Dow plummeted. By the time the markets closed, it was a bloodbath. Billions of dollars in equity were lost.

The evening news warned that if more money weren't made available it was possible that the market could collapse. The previous pessimists warned of a drop of 50 percent or more in the market. The previous optimists argued for a less severe drop of 20 to 25 percent.

What bothered Jerry was the lack of support for any significant uptick. Market fears were now predicted to bring millions of additional sellers into the market Monday morning and early results in foreign markets showed a stampede to sell "tech" stocks at any price. A few hours after the market opened, all trading was suspended in a truly unprecedented move to try to halt the panic.

The president made a speech that evening and told Americans that the fundamentals were sound and the market would recover. The next day, when the bell rang on Wall Street, hordes of media were on hand to watch. Within 10 minutes the trend was set. Massive selling by individual investors flooded the market. By noon the market was in free fall: down nearly 50 percent.

Market managers could only sit and watch as equities plunged. The preset trading limits prohibited their trades. Countless billions of dollars evaporated in the greatest retreat in market history. Jerry watched as his "easy money" disappeared, then his "real" money went with it. He knew he was wiped out. He didn't even keep enough cash to pay this month's bills. He was angry. *But at whom?* he thought. *The doomsdayers,* he decided. *They caused this with their stupid pessimism.*

Jerry is a fictitious name, but his story—including everything from the drop in U.S. exports to the soaring technology stocks—is based on real-life facts and events. And lest you assume that Jerry is modeled on someone you know, I want to let you in on a little secret. Jerry was born in 1892, and the trades he was making were on October 26, 1929—just three days before the crash that triggered the Great Depression.

Then and Now

It's been said that he who fails to learn from the past is doomed to repeat it. With that in mind, I want to take a step back and look at the political and economic climate in the U.S. just prior to the Great Depression.

As Jerry noted, high-tech stocks were all the rage. The new industrial revolution, which moved into high gear in the first two decades of the 20th century, unified the country and made communication more efficient than ever before. Wireless telegraphy, invented in the 1890s, paved the way for voice-carrying radio, which came loud and clear into American homes in 1921. The Radio Corporation of America (RCA) brought broadcast radio to America. In 1922 RCA sold for 85 times earnings but was more in line at 36 times earnings by 1929. (Today AOL, Yahoo! and eBay sell for 577:1, 569:1, and 3,324:1 respectively.)

With the huge success of technology stocks and the money they attracted, it opened the doors to new "miracles," such as transatlantic wireless photographs, radiotelephones, and television.

Radio waves weren't the only things flying through the airways. In 1927, Charles Lindbergh dazzled the world by piloting his single-engine plane, *The Spirit of St. Louis,* from New York to Paris—a heroic feat that sent America's can-do spirit soaring and ignited the brand new aviation industry.

And on the ground, the prosperity was infectious as muddy trails gave way to hard-surface roads. By 1929 the nation's burgeoning highway network carried 26 million automobiles (one car for every 4.9 Americans[1]), courtesy of Henry Ford and his ilk.

If any brokerage houses had offered "science and technology" funds, they would have been runaway winners. As it was, stock prices for radio, television, and other electronics easily outpaced other issues—much like today's Internet stocks have carried the day. The parallels to the '20s market are remarkable.

But the economic similarities between the pre-Depression era and today range far beyond the climate on Wall Street. For one thing, consumer debt was a new and very popular phenomenon in the 1920s. With the advent of installment-plan financing, a tight cash flow proved no obstacle to automobile ownership, and countless Americans began driving cars that they didn't own. And as average consumers watched money merchants getting wealthy in the stock market, they looked to the bankers for investment capital. With loans often carrying interest rates of 20 percent or more, the bankers realized incredible profits and then began easing loan qualifications to attract even more borrowers.

Sound familiar? At the beginning of this book I told you that many of the callers to our radio program were heavily invested in the stock market and heavily leveraged on their credit cards. Investors haven't changed, and neither have the bankers. With credit cards in use in 80 percent of American households, card issuers have lowered their requirements and cranked up their direct mail campaigns. In 1997, they sent out a record 3 billion credit card solicitations; and a growing number of offers are going to households with incomes of less than $20,000 per year.[2]

The economic similarities go on and on. In the late 1920s, just like in the 1990s, America surged ahead of the rest of the world in productivity and prosperity. Just about the only people who didn't benefit from the industrial improvements were farmers, who found themselves facing agricultural surpluses and sagging prices (an almost identical scenario to today: farmers can barely sell their produce at a profit, and ranchers can't recover the cost of feeding their livestock). Farmers' complaints helped usher in the Hawley-Smoot Tariff of 1930, which morphed into the highest protective tariff in the nation's peacetime history, raising import tariff rates to nearly 60 percent.

To our trading partners overseas, still reeling from the financial upheaval of World War I, the move was nothing short of economic warfare. Within a year, 25 foreign countries had taken retaliatory action against the U.S. by erecting tariffs of their own. The U.S. was plunged into economic isolationism.

Perhaps former U.S. Treasury Secretary Robert Rubin had that scenario in mind when, earlier this year, he warned that the world economy was becoming dangerously dependent on the U.S. for growth. As our trade deficit soared and exports fell for the first time in 13 years (while cheaper imports continued to rise), the talk on Capitol Hill has been of shielding the nation by imposing protectionist measures (higher tariffs). But, as Rubin pointed out, "If we look as if we're closing our market, that would set off protectionist pressures around the world."[3]

In April 1999, the Fed chairman issued a verbal warning that protectionist talk was "very dangerous." Dr. Greenspan may well have been making reference to the "great banana war" between the U.S. and the European Community (EC).

Because of tariffs placed on U.S. bananas going into the EC, the U.S. imposed 100 percent duty taxes on $191 million worth of imported goods from the EC. The EC countered with a ban on hormone-treated U.S. beef, and then the U.S. threatened to ban hundreds of millions of dollars worth of products from the EC. When the EC defiantly added virtually all of the older, noisier U.S. jets to its airport ban, the U.S. threatened to ban the Concorde (supersonic jet) from U.S. airports.[4] And that's how trade wars get started!

Perhaps the most sobering parallel between the 1920s era and now is the optimism that pervades our culture. As I write this, economists have been raising their growth forecasts for the foreseeable future. "The market," they say, "is supported by a wonderful economic environment." Pointing to the billions of dollars that baby boomers continue to pump into the market through automatic contributions to 401(k) plans and other mutual funds, Hugh Johnson, a strategist at First Albany, fully expects stock prices to double in the next seven years.[5]

Reading comments like these, I can't help but recall Herbert Hoover's acceptance speech after he was elected to the presidency in 1928: he implied that America was nearer to the final triumph over poverty than ever before in the history of our land. If I recall correctly, he said something like, "The poorhouse is vanishing. We are in sight of the day when poverty will be banished from this nation."

Less than one year later, Americans were facing bread lines for the first time in history. Ex-millionaires were jumping out of office buildings, and investors who had been assured that the fundamentals were sound had lost some $40 billion in equity in the market—more than the United States' total cost of World War I.

The Recession: Can We Avoid It?

Having drawn all these parallels, am I now predicting another Great Depression? Who knows? I surely don't, but most think probably not. The one really positive factor is that history seldom, if ever, repeats similar scenarios. Therefore, the very fact that current events seem to conform so well to those of the past will alert too many bright people for them to allow another Depression (or at least I hope so). However, it is important to note here that what touched off the Depression in 1929 were not any real problems within American companies. In fact, American businesses were doing quite well. U.S. Steel and the automotive companies had just had record years. RCA and GE were also having banner years. Jobs were abundant, and the flapper generation was living it up.

As I said, the new innovation of consumer credit had made it possible for average-income families to own cars, radios, stoves, even iceboxes in which perishable foods could be kept for days. All forms of credit had become a national pastime, along with stock market speculation.

It was the public's fascination with credit-financed investing, and the panic that ensued when the bankers cut off that credit supply, that probably sparked the first big market run. Just like today, investors in the Roaring Twenties saw themselves and their booming economy as virtually invulnerable. When the cracks appeared, most were caught unaware (but not everyone).

A headline from the *New York Times* (October 16, 1929, less than two weeks before the crash) quoted one of the leading optimists/economists of the day, Dr. Irving Fisher, Yale University: **"Fisher Sees Stocks Permanently High."** Professor of Business Dr. Amos Dice (at Ohio State University, a leading business consultant of that period) is quoted, **"Stock Prices Will Stay at High Level for Years to Come."**

In the *New York Times*, October 15, 1929: **"Moody's** [stock rating service] **sees stock rise justified."** Byline: **"Moody's says returns are in line with industrial activity."**

There were some sober voices in the crowd. In July, the *New York Times* quoted noted statistician, Dr. Roger Babson, who spoke at the 16th National Business Conference. He predicted an imminent stock market crash caused by unreasonable investor speculation. To a large degree, his concerns were ridiculed and ignored. Several other noted financial analysts had been saying virtually the same thing for at least two years. Of course, with proponents on both sides, someone will be right and someone will be wrong.

The major factor in doing any serious economic analysis is *timing*. We are all biased by our perceptions and tend to underestimate the resilience of the American economy. But to be honest and to live with ourselves, whether we are pessimists, optimists, or realists, we have to call it the way we see it.

In actuality, the historical facts supported Dr. Babson's position. A "bubble" had developed that eventually burst on Thursday, October 27, 1929. The stock market ultimately lost $40 billion (the equivalent of nearly $1 trillion today) in equity, and the Roaring Twenties came to an end.

The market had several rallies as brokers and businessmen tried to stem the tide (as the old saying goes); but all they accomplished was to wreck their own personal finances. Once a "bubble" bursts—like the tulip mania, the South Sea Islands, or the Mississippi Delta—no amount of persuasion, cash, or words—will restore confidence.

The trillion dollar question today is, "Has another bubble developed?"

It is *not* my opinion that we are headed for a depression. Instead, I think that in the year 2000, even without Y2K-related problems, we are scheduled for a significant economic/market slowdown. In my opinion—and remember, that's all I can offer: an *opinion*—we will likely see an economic downturn triggered by the recession that is engulfing most of the world today. It is impossible to tell whether the economy will spark a market sell-off or if a stock market sell-off will deflate the economy. Either is possible.

With Asia, Europe, and Latin America all struggling with recession—and, in some cases, economic collapse—our current growth pattern is simply not sustainable. An honest look at our rising trade deficit is, all by itself, enough to take some of the air out of this bubble. How much? That's a good question.

The U.S. trade deficit (the amount we import over what we export) is now running over $17 billion a *month!* A few years ago that would have been nearly half a year's trade deficit. And the trend is getting worse, and it will until other nations' economies improve.[6]

Our trade conflicts with the EC can turn mean very quickly, given the current administration's tendency to shoot themselves in the foot. Europe alone accounts for 28 percent of U.S. exports and 15 percent of U.S. corporate profits. Latin America accounts for another 20 percent, and their economies (and currencies) are in the *pits*.[7] Japan is in the midst of a prolonged recession, and Indonesia and Micronesia have virtually collapsed.

As Federal Chairman Greenspan told Congress in early 1999, the U.S. is virtually alone among the world's top economies. As previously noted, he warned Congress: "The U.S. cannot remain an oasis of prosperity in a world economy racked by financial distress."[8] So far, Dr. Greenspan has not been right; however, it's quite possible that he will be vindicated in the year 2000.

As the president of the National Association of Manufacturers said, "We're really concerned about later this year, and in particular 2000.... Half the world is in recession, and there is overcapacity in most of the rest of the world. Europe is slowing and is not likely to be as strong. And Brazil is on the edge of a national disaster."[9]

In addition to a world economic recession, we have the twin problems of our individual and national debt loads, coupled with a dangerously anemic savings rate. The average American currently saves nothing in any cash reserve (in fact, less than nothing). The average family has no financial security in the event of a job loss or other financial crisis.

I talk with these people every day. They are educated, intelligent Christians who live on the brink of financial disaster. Why? Because that's how they have been taught. They borrowed tens of thousands of dollars to go to college, more thousands on credit cards to entertain while they were in college, and multiple thousands more to get established after graduation. In my state, they are told to play the lottery as a retirement plan.

The stock market to them is just another lottery. If they lose even one week's salary, they cannot pay their basic bills (mortgage, cars, food, utilities). It has been my observation that it is not uncommon for one of these average American families to accumulate *$50,000 or more* in credit card debt when between jobs!

You just wait until the next economic downturn. I believe we will see financial crisis on a scale never imagined by previous generations. This will have an effect on our economy. We'll discover that the rules haven't changed all that much. When people don't have money to spend, the economy constricts and everyone—from businesses to the government—feels the pinch.

So, What's Really Going to Happen?

Add to this volatile mix the fact that, by historical standards, our economy is overdue for a correction and you have a realistic potential for trouble. As I said earlier, based on traditional measurements and values, the Dow Jones Industrial Average should be at about 4,400. Instead, it recently blew past the 11,000 mark and possibly will climb even higher before this book is published (especially if the economy experiences a pre-Y2K mini-boom from businesses stocking up on essential inventories in the latter half of this year).

Which brings us back to Y2K. Even though the computer glitch alone may not be enough to trigger a full-scale recession, the fear factor that already has people withdrawing cash from their banks, selling off stocks, and hoarding everything from toilet paper to tuna fish very possibly will set the stage for a stagnant economy in the new year. And if, as we saw earlier, federal services or private corporations shut down—even temporarily—"stagnant" will not describe the situation. Confidence, like integrity, is slow to develop and fast to dissolve.

So What Should You Do If . . .

We're heading for a recession?

The stock market takes a dive?

Y2K turns out to be worse than you thought?

If consumer confidence declines, should you take your money out of the stock market? It depends. Consumer confidence really measures the probability that average households will react a certain way. If confidence is high, they're expected to spend more, borrow more, and take more risks. If confidence is low, they're expected to spend less, pay back debt, and generally conserve.

Measuring consumer confidence is an inexact science. I believe we reached the peak in '98 and confidence has been eroding ever since. I saw this confidence gap begin in '99, when our callers stopped asking about the stock market and started asking about how to get out of debt! I believe as consumer confidence fades more and more people will become skittish about the stock market and their jobs.

It's important to realize that you can make money in any economy, or in any market. It really depends on how you view the changes. If you think the market will drop and you short it, you win, even though stock values go down.

How each of us responds to market changes depends on a variety of factors, including age, financial goals, and a personal tolerance for risk. We'll take a closer look at investor temperaments and risk tolerance in the last half of this book. For now, though, let's look at how investment strategies can differ, depending on age and financial goals.

If you are 40 or younger, I recommend that you not focus on short-term cycles in the economy or the stock market, unless they directly affect your income. A market decline may be very important if you're a broker or a financial planner, managing other people's money. But unless the economy falls into another depression, the stock market is still the place to make the best return. The market represents the world's largest economy.

Obviously it would be better to avoid the market downturns, if possible. There is methodology to do this, known as market timing. Market timing is an inexact science, as we'll discuss in a later section. Market timing is not for the faint of heart.

A point should be made that if enough people react negatively to a major downturn in the stock market (or the economy) it can easily create a crisis. Whether or not Y2K is a real problem, panic can make it real enough. Some people have voiced a concern that by writing this book I might manipulate the market. Not to worry; that I cannot do. I am concerned that God's people understand the risks we face in this economy and then make intelligent, educated choices.

The tendency, because the "bears" have been wrong in their forecasts of a downturn (so far), is to believe that it cannot or will not happen. That is a very naive philosophy. If you cannot manage a prolonged market downturn—financially, emotionally, or by virtue of your age—don't wait until such a crisis occurs. It will be too late. Take your profits and/or your investment capital, and run! Now! The most you can lose are the taxes you will owe anyway and a few months' potential profits.

I'd like to share what I have personally done to prepare, in light of what I believe is coming.

In July of 1998, I cashed out 70 percent of all market positions (i.e., stocks, mutual funds). I didn't feel comfortable having all of our long-term assets in the market. But, because I also didn't want to miss what appeared to be a once-in-a-lifetime market bubble, I left 30 percent invested and even bought some "tulip bulbs" or, in this case, some Internet stocks. As these stocks have grown (wildly and ridiculously), I sold off enough to get my initial investment out, which I reinvested in sound, mainline companies like GE, GM, and Coke.

As long as this bubble economy survives, I will continue to benefit and pull out capital periodically. But when this parade stops, and I believe it will, I won't lose more than I can absorb—mostly profits, not earned income. This concept works for me, but you need to decide on one that works for you. My investment guide is usually sleep. If I can't sleep, I don't invest.

If you opt to stay invested in the stock market, follow the dictates of common sense when it comes to deciding which stocks to buy. Companies that require a high volume of exports, for example, or that have a high percentage of Asian suppliers, are probably not wise choices right now. Also, although the Internet may be hot today, one *Forbes* magazine contributor recently predicted that 80 to 85 percent of these stocks could fail within the next five years. Whether this is right or not, before you sink your paycheck (i.e., real money) into any high-tech offerings, step back and take a reality check.

If you're thinking about borrowing to invest, go to the library and check out a copy of *Security Analysis*, a 1934 classic by

Benjamin Graham and David Dodd. (This is one of billionaire Warren Buffett's favorite books.) Graham and Dodd, in reviewing the '29 market collapse, concluded that investors, rather than relying on traditional investment fundamentals like assets and capital, developed new-era ideas—ideas that argued that the value of a common stock "depends entirely on what it *may* earn in the future." (Sound familiar?)

Graham and Dodd concluded that the line between speculation and investment faded and that the actual price of a stock was irrelevant in deciding whether it was a good buy (shades of Amazon.com).[10]

In general, I like Warren Buffett's take on investing: When you buy the leader in any industry, you buy quality. In a negative economy, fundamentals matter, and industry leading companies will outlast the "hotshot" upstarts.

The information provided by a friend at a major car company is a case in point. Though smaller companies may flounder in a Y2K-generated recession, powerhouses like GM and Ford will have the resources to buy out both suppliers and competitors, thereby strengthening their own financial positions. In short, if you are going to put money you have earned into the market, put it with the proven winners.

And above all, don't panic. After this economic crisis comes and goes (as it must), the ensuing recovery period should leave our economy stronger than ever. The key goal is to make it through the down times without losing everything you have worked for.

I believe that those who cannot ride out a multiyear economic downturn should withdraw whatever portion of their assets necessary to make them feel at peace. As I shared, in my case it was 70 percent. Was it worth the taxes paid? Yes, for me it was. I used some of the appreciated stocks to do my charitable giving, which reduced the tax burden somewhat, and some of the sales were in tax-sheltered IRAs.

So, What's Really Going to Happen?

Have I missed some potential profits by getting out when I did? Most assuredly. The 30 percent I still have in the market has raised the entire principal amount to an average yield of 21 percent over the last two years. If it had all been in the same stocks, the yield could have been a staggering 172 percent!

Do I regret my decision to be cautious? Not at all. It fits my age, my temperament, and my goals. After all, I could have remortgaged our home, maxed out our credit cards, and raised the yield to maybe 300 percent. Would I do so even if I believed the next two years would duplicate the last two? Not a chance! I believe, having looked at a lot of data, that 2000 and beyond are going to bring on big economic changes—some bad, in the short run.

But only God knows the future. If you shift some assets and the timing is off and 2000 isn't the year for the *big* correction, all you'll miss are some profits. You can always switch back into the market by mid-2000. If my analysis (feelings, guess, whatever) is correct, you'll miss a major market and economy correction.

I'll have to be honest here and say I'm not sure how much of what I "feel" is based on the hyperventilating stock market and how much is based on a desire to see God bring this nation to its knees. The U.S. economy is poised for a *major* downturn, and Americans need to fear God once again; and maybe these two events will coincide.

I believe God wants to help His people who obey His rules. In the next section of this book, I'll give you the principles you need to do just that.

---

1. Thomas A. Bailey, *The American Pageant* (Lexington: D.C. Heath and Co., 1975), 852.
2. Nancy Stancill, "Congratulations! You're Our Newest Customer," *Charlotte Observer*, October 18, 1998, 10A.

3. Rich Miller, "U.S. Economy a Bubble Waiting to Burst," *USA Today*, March 11, 1999, 1A–2A.

4. "U.S. tariff plan wins approval; EC may dig in," *USA Today*, April 20, 1999, 1B.

5. David Rynecki, "Dow vs. forces of gravity," *USA Today*, March 30, 1999, 3B.

6. Beth Bolton, "January trade deficit hits record $17B," *USA Today*, March 19, 1999.

7. *USA Today*, March 11, 1999.

8. Ibid.

9. *Chicago Tribune*, March 17, 1999.

10. Herb Greenburg, *Fortune* magazine, October 1997.

PART II

SEVEN KEYS TO EFFECTIVE INVESTING
FOR THE NEW MILLENNIUM

8

Principle One:
Establish Short-Term Goals

John set up his first lemonade stand just after his birthday in 1972. He charged his customers 10 cents per cup and, after deducting the $1.79 he had spent on paper cups and lemonade mix, he realized a profit of $2.21. Not bad, he figured, for an afternoon's work. He already knew how he would spend his fortune: He planned to give 10 percent to his Sunday school class, spend another $1.50 on a birthday present for his mother, and stash the rest in his piggy bank until he had enough to buy his own baseball glove.

Nearly two decades later, John earned his Ph.D. in economics from a prestigious East Coast university. As he contemplated this achievement, John's thoughts returned to his first career. He realized he had learned more about things like budgeting, saving, and goal-setting through his lemonade stand than he had ever picked up in college or graduate school!

John's experience is not at all uncommon. You can go from elementary school through one of the nation's finest universities without ever learning basic skills, such as how to balance a checkbook, buy a home, or set financial goals.

Most Americans don't live on a budget—at least not in the true sense of the word.

When we say that a new set of golf clubs isn't "in our budget," what we really mean is that we don't have the cash to buy them. Budgeting, in our modern vocabulary, is a lot like dieting: both are last-resort measures we rely on when it's time to tighten the belt a notch or two.

I know of one couple who used what they called "Budget Restriction" when they wanted to buy something they couldn't afford. If the item was particularly expensive, they went into a mode called "Secret Budget Restriction." And when they wanted to buy something really big, such as a house, they instituted "Double Secret Budget Restriction." I have no idea what all these code words really meant; all I know is that each successive phase signaled another reduction in their spending.

For them, the concept of budgeting had very little to do with financial planning; instead, it amounted to a temporary cutback in living expenses. All too often decisions are made with a short-term view. For instance, a couple will decide to lease a car because they lack a down payment to finance one (and never have the cash to buy one). This plan works somewhat the first year, when the car is new and under warranty; but, when the tires wear out and other repairs are necessary, their so-called budget fails.

In reality, a budget is a short-term tool that you can use to achieve long-term goals. It is a spending plan to help you allocate money with an eye toward avoiding debt and saving for future needs. I'm not going to focus on the mechanics of budgeting in this book; if you want that information, please see my workbook entitled *The Financial Planning Workbook* (Moody Press, 1990). Rather, I want us to consider the long-term side of the equation: goal setting.

Goal setting is a chief prerequisite to effective investing. As you consider what you want to do with your money in the new millennium, you need to think about where you want to wind up—financially. In the short term, you need to decide whether you want to ride out the downturn that Y2K is likely to cause to duck the effects by shifting assets. Or maybe some combination will fit your temperament better—as it does mine. I have some very specific financial goals that I'll call "life goals." In this chapter we will look at some of the most common financial "destination points": lifestyle choices, saving goals, and giving goals.

Obviously, everyone's goals will be different. Our backgrounds and temperaments affect the way we live today, and your financial needs and wants will not be the same as mine, nor will they always line up perfectly with your spouse's. What you'll need to do is find a reasonable compromise.

Goal Setting

All of our goals must have two things in common. First, they must be *written*; second, they must be *biblical.*

Almost all of us, I suspect, would agree that written goals are more apt to be achieved than the dreams and ideas that remain in our heads, but few people ever take the time to actually commit their plans to paper. In this chapter you will have the opportunity to establish at least four financial goals. Talk and pray with your spouse about each area, and make a list of your goals.

The second common denominator is God's Word. The Bible does not offer an individualized plan for how we are to use our money, but God does give us principles we can rely on as we make our plans. For instance, in Proverbs we read, *"By wisdom a house is built, and by understanding it is established; and by knowledge the rooms are filled with all precious and pleasant riches"* (Proverbs 24:3–4).

Set your goals. Then ask God for wisdom. Read the Bible, looking for goal-setting nuggets, such as this one: *"Do not weary yourself to gain wealth, cease from your consideration of it. When you set your eyes on it, it is gone. For wealth certainly makes itself wings, like an eagle that flies toward the heavens*" (Proverbs 23:4–5). This principle sounds simple, but the ability to show restraint cannot be underestimated, especially when it comes to setting limits on your lifestyle.

Goal #1: Control Your Spending

Sir John Templeton founded the Templeton Fund, one of the most successful mutual fund companies in the world. For several decades, countless investors have looked to him for financial advice. Today he is one of the world's wealthiest men. But that was not always true. Templeton grew up in a poor family and knew, firsthand, the real value of money.

When Templeton began to earn a salary, he resolved to give generously, spend modestly, and invest wisely. As he prospered, he purposed to use whatever money he made to help other people. Today the Templeton Prize for Progress in Religion, a financial award in excess of $1,000,000, is given to innovators in the field of religion. It is just another evidence of his generosity. What is the secret to his phenomenal philanthropic career?[1]

You say it is his money? You think that anyone with a few hundred million dollars to spare can be a philanthropist. Right? Perhaps, but not everyone who has the money is so willing to share it. In fact, statistics show that the more money you make, the smaller percentage of it you give away. If giving habits are not established as a result of spiritual conviction, giving actually declines with more money. Why? Because there are more things to do with it.

Christ told His disciples about the rich young ruler: *"Jesus looked at him and said, 'How hard it is for those who are wealthy to enter the kingdom of God!'"* (Luke 18:24).

What makes John Templeton so different? I believe his success—both in accumulating wealth and in sharing it with others—has to do with his value system and with the self-imposed limits he maintains in his lifestyle. His house, for example, is not much bigger than it was before he made his fortune. Likewise, you don't read about Templeton having 14 Porsches in his garage—although he certainly could afford them. John Templeton knows when enough is enough.

Paul J. Meyer is another millionaire who came from a financially impoverished background. He founded a company called Success Motivation Institute and owns more than a dozen companies doing business worldwide. Like Templeton, Meyer decided early on to become debt free. He adopted a conservative lifestyle, buying used furniture and driving secondhand cars. He put himself on a fixed income and reinvested his money in people, rather than things. Today he has chosen to give millions into God's work rather than raise the bar on his own spending as his wealth has increased.

Make no mistake: John Templeton and Paul Meyer live well—better, probably, than most average Americans. But they do not live ostentatiously, and they certainly don't live as well as their great wealth would allow. I am convinced that when they stand before the Lord on Judgment Day, they will not have to apologize for how they have used their resources. The same could have been said of R.G. LeTourneau, J.C. Penney, and countless other men and women who were blessed with the ability to create wealth.

The servants of God who have been blessed with wealth have many traits in common, chief among which may be their resolve, *before* they made their millions, to settle the question of "How much is enough?"

Not everyone has so much foresight. I recall a Christian businessman who built a very successful business. During his working career he paid himself a $100,000 salary—a modest amount, considering what his company was worth. Eventually, he sold the business for more than $30 million. He was committed to tithing, so he gave away $5 million—a sizable sum. Later, he asked a Christian friend if he thought he should have given more.

"Well, how much did you used to live on?" his friend asked.

"About $100,000 a year."

"Well," his friend commented, "if you took $2 million and put it in a bond fund, it would pay you at least that much every year, wouldn't it?"

"Yes," he agreed, "it would."

"So why don't you do that and give the rest away? After all, what are you going to do with $20 million?"

The businessman paused and then came back with a list of unforeseen expenses that could negatively impact his lifestyle, if they actually happened. "I would need some more reserve," he argued.

"Okay," his friend conceded. "Take the $2 million and double it. Put $4 million aside. Now you'll have $200,000 a year—twice as much money to live on as you used to."

"Yes, but. . . ." It's easy to see what this committed Christian businessman was up against. Having sold his business for several million dollars, he had adjusted his sights to a higher level: beach houses, mountain getaways, several million dollars of inheritance money for each of the children, travel plans, and on and on. As his dreams mushroomed, the money he might have used for kingdom purposes was whittled down to a minority portion. And it's easy to criticize him, looking in from the outside. But what if God gave you the ability to earn a million dollars a year? Or $10 million? Would it be enough? At what point would you decide how much is enough?

Unless you settle the question of how much is enough before you have the money in hand, you will never be satisfied with your lifestyle. There are always more ways to spend money. Even if you suddenly found yourself with multiple millions, you could convince yourself that it isn't enough.

There is an end to my story. After a lot of prayer, the businessman and his wife decided to keep only a tithe from the business sale and gave 90 percent away. A little over a year later they were both killed when the private plane in which they were flying crashed. Their decision was the right one—for eternity!

So how much is enough? The Bible does not provide a specific answer to this question. Different people have different limits. I have one friend who lives in a multimillion dollar home. I would not be comfortable living there (even if I could afford it!), but he and his wife are at peace about it. More importantly, he is completely comfortable living there *before the Lord*—and considering how often they use their home to help Christian groups and visiting missionaries, few could find fault with their lifestyle. It reflects their Christianity very well.

If you are in the 50-plus category, your age group is said to have more discretionary income than any other segment of our society. Here are some facts to consider as you plan your retirement lifestyle and the way you will pass on your estate to your survivors—in what economists claim will be the greatest transfer of wealth in the history of the world.

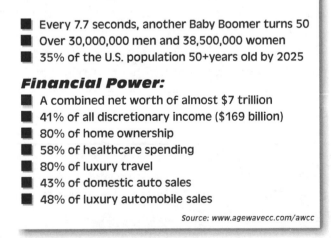

Our "Fifty+Plus" Population

- Every 7.7 seconds, another Baby Boomer turns 50
- Over 30,000,000 men and 38,500,000 women
- 35% of the U.S. population 50+years old by 2025

Financial Power:
- A combined net worth of almost $7 trillion
- 41% of all discretionary income ($169 billion)
- 80% of home ownership
- 58% of healthcare spending
- 80% of luxury travel
- 43% of domestic auto sales
- 48% of luxury automobile sales

Source: www.agewavecc.com/awcc

When Judy and I set our lifestyle goals years ago, we set goals to pay off our home, educate our children, buy each of them their first car, and give them $20,000 toward their first home. Besides those things, we wanted to have money available to meet unforeseen needs (such as when our son needed a loan to help start his business, or when our daughter's husband walked out and she found herself with no income and a young son to raise on her own). We also wanted to have enough money invested so that if something happened to me Judy would have adequate resources for the rest of her life.

Having established our lifestyle parameters, we calculated how much money we would need to meet these expenses. Today, we have paid off our home, "launched" our children, and met most of our lifestyle goals; and we know that any extra money that comes in, therefore, is not meant for us to keep. But if we hadn't set our goals *before* we made any money, we might have had a tough time limiting our lifestyle, especially in a booming economy.

As you consider your own lifestyle limits, pray about your options. What kind of a home should you live in? What kind of vacations will you take? What schools will your children attend? Recognize that your resources—your money, your home, your business—all belong to God. They are tools you can use in God's kingdom. He doesn't care how much or how little things cost. What counts in His eyes is the attitude of your heart.

Talk and pray with your spouse about the "How much is enough?" issue, and set some goals that reflect your individual lifestyle parameters. By setting these goals now, you will be better equipped to resist the temptation to raise the bar as your assets increase. Moreover, by restricting your lifestyle and reining in your spending, you will be better prepared to help others when the need arises.

Get a piece of paper and, as you and your family discuss these questions, write the answers. Feel free to add to or revise this list as you consider your family's individual needs and set goals in these areas.

1. How much will we spend on housing, currently and as our children grow?

2. What kinds of cars will we drive, and what will they cost? How often will we replace them?

3. Where will we go on vacation, and how much will we spend each year?

4. How much will it cost to educate our children? Will they attend private/Christian schools?

5. How much are we willing to spend on college costs?

6. How much money, as a percentage of our income, will we give to our church or other charitable/Christian organizations? As our income rises, will we increase this amount?

7. What other lifestyle goals do we have?

Goal #2: Determine Your Debt Tolerance

Another important goal-setting area revolves around debt. How much debt, if any, should you have? More specifically, how much debt should you have as we move into the economic uncertainties of the new millennium? If you lost your job or were forced to take a pay cut, how much debt could you handle?

My own debt-tolerance level is close to zero. But that is a personal conviction. The Bible doesn't prohibit borrowing; it establishes specific limits on borrowing. As with lifestyle limits, the biblical wisdom regarding debt levels does not come in a one-size-fits-all format. Rather, I think the Lord gives us reasonable boundaries within which we can operate.

When it comes to debt, the minimum boundary is found in verses like this one: *"The wicked borrows and does not pay back"* (Psalm 37:21). In other words, if you borrow money, you are obligated to pay it back. As Christians, we cannot take on debt that we have no reasonable expectation of repaying. If you get to the point in your borrowing that you sacrifice your own reputation or jeopardize your family's financial position because you cannot repay a loan, you are beyond God's limit.

On the upper end of the borrowing spectrum, the biblical principle is that you should be able to lend money to those in need, including those who can never repay you. *"If you lend to those from whom you expect to receive, what credit is that to you? Even sinners lend to sinners, in order to receive back the same amount"* (Luke 6:34). If you are in debt to the point that you're not able to lend to the needy, then you are operating outside of God's design.

In a marriage relationship, husbands and wives often have vastly different debt-tolerance levels. Typically (and this is admittedly a generalization), a woman is far less comfortable with indebtedness than her husband is. She sees debt as a burden; he sees it as a necessary means to achieve their goals.

Don and Karen came to see me because Karen was frantic over his level of indebtedness. While attending medical school, they had run up nearly $150,000 in school loans. Don had finished his residency and had joined a five-person obstetrics practice. With an income in excess of $125,000 a year, Karen felt like they should pay down their debts. Instead Don opted to borrow to buy a bigger home and borrowed to invest in some real estate deals with his partners.

"I can make enough money on these two deals to pay off the school loans," he told me.

"But what if you don't?" Karen argued. "I want to get *out* of debt—not get in further." After several more sessions, Don reluctantly agreed to get out of the investments and concentrate on paying down their debts.

Barely two years later Don was diagnosed with leukemia. He received extensive chemo treatments and a bone-marrow transplant, but he died three years later. At the time of his death they were totally debt free (after selling their house) and Karen had enough money to relocate and finish her nursing degree. She has often shared how being debt free helped her cope with Don's death and being faced with raising two children alone.

Remember, debt can be an anchor, but it will never be a life preserver.

If you are married, talk with your spouse about your debt-tolerance level. Find out what the Bible says about debt by reading passages such as Proverbs 3:27; 6:1-5; 11:15; 17:18; 20:16; 22:7. If your current debt load exceeds your personal comfort level, talk and pray about ways to reduce it. As I mentioned earlier, Christian Financial Concepts has trained counselors who can help you get out of debt; the phone number is 770-534-1000.

Goal #3: How Much Can You Save?

A third goal to establish is how much money you plan to save—either a specific dollar amount or a percentage of what you earn. Thomas Stanley and William Danko wrote a book, *The Millionaire Next Door* (Longstreet Press, 1996), in which they asserted that most American millionaires are difficult to identify. They don't drive flashy cars; they don't live in the most upscale neighborhoods; and the vast majority of them have earned, rather than inherited, their money.

Based on surveys of more than 11,000 high-net-worth and/or high-income people, the authors point to several common denominators among those who have managed to build and maintain their wealth. First among these traits is that affluent people live well below their means, rejecting the big-spending lifestyles most of us associate with rich people. Another common characteristic among the truly wealthy is a compulsion to save and invest regularly.

While reading *The Millionaire Next Door*, I couldn't help but think about a pastor I met years ago at a missions conference in California. He approached me after one of my money management seminars and asked if we could meet. "I have a real financial problem," he said, "and I'd like to talk with you about it."

I guessed that the pastor was about 75 years old. Since I knew that the highest salary in his organization was about $10,000 a year, it wasn't hard to imagine his problem: Facing retirement, he was undoubtedly flat broke and he had no idea, I assumed, how he would survive when he could no longer earn his meager salary.

Boy, was I in for a surprise. As it turned out, the pastor had several hundred thousand dollars in savings. "Plus," he confided, "I have several pieces of land worth that much or more. We also have our home and two cars debt free. My problem is this: I don't need the money or the property, and I'm wondering what I should do with it."

I was flabbergasted. (So much for my assumptions!) "Where did you get all that money?" I asked.

"I just saved it up," he replied, as though saving a few hundred thousand dollars was the most natural thing in the world. "I never spent more than I made, I always lived on less, and I always took 10 percent of whatever I earned and put it into savings. I used some of the money to buy land."

I knew that the pastors at the conference typically did not stay in one town for more than three years or so. Their focus was on church planting, and once a church was well established, the pastor usually moved on to a new location. What he had done, I learned, was to purchase property when he moved into town and then sell it a few years later when he left. He did not set out to make a fortune; rather, he simply focused on the principle of saving money and investing it on a regular basis—a habit he maintained for 40 years.

This pastor's story illustrates one of the most important principles of sound financial management: It is not the *amount* of money you earn that matters, but how *diligent* you are about spending less than you earn and saving the excess.

I saw this principle played out over and over when I was counseling several professional athletes. The athletes who came out of their careers with plenty of money were generally the same ones who refrained from buying pricey homes and fancy new cars.

Steve Largent is a case in point. His teammates on the Seattle Seahawks used to laugh at how humble his cars looked compared to theirs. But Largent had the last laugh: When he quit playing football, he had socked away enough money to do whatever he wanted to for the rest of his life. Today he serves in the U.S. Congress—at a fraction of his former salary.

Again, it doesn't matter whether you make $10,000 a year (like the itinerant pastor I talked with) or $10 million (like professional athletes do today). What makes a difference in your long-term financial security is your willingness to save rather than to spend. Consider the wisdom: *"There is precious treasure and oil in the dwelling of the wise, but a foolish man swallows it up"* (Proverbs 21:20).

If my sense about the timing of the coming recession is correct, you may not have the opportunity to set aside a large sum of money before the downturn hits. But every dollar you save today is a dollar that will be available to you tomorrow. And by establishing a savings habit now, you can meet the new millennium (and whatever financial future it brings) in a position to build, rather than squander, your wealth.

How much money will you purpose to save? If you are not already saving, start by setting aside some percentage of your take-home pay. I'll tell you how to invest your savings in a later chapter; for now, the main thing is to make saving some amount a priority. The greater the income, the greater the percentage should be (after your giving, of course).

Goal #4: How Much Should You Give?

Perhaps the most important goal-setting area, especially for Christians, is how much you want to give to God's kingdom. Judy became a Christian three years before I did. At the time, I worked at the Cape Canaveral Space Center with some of the world's top scientists, and I tended to scoff at Christianity. I saw it as a religion for people who were weak. Certainly giving to anything was not in my priority system. I loved Judy, but there was no way that I was going to give any of our money to the church, no matter how much she wanted me to. "After all," I told her, "they have a bigger building than I do."

Then when I finally decided to give my life to Christ, my outlook changed dramatically. Suddenly, I wanted to give *everything* away: our money, our home, our possessions, everything! I look back and realize that my fanaticism must have really unnerved Judy. But strong as it was, my impulsive generosity was not motivated by compassion or any desire to honor or obey God. Rather, I wanted to give to assuage my guilt. Having mocked God for years, I hoped to win His favor by giving Him all that I had. The only problem was, I didn't know if even that would be "enough."

Obviously, no amount of money can buy God's grace; if it could, Christ's death would have been pointless. Yet my early desire to give God everything raises an important question: How much is enough, when it comes to giving?

Once again, Scripture offers no clear-cut answer. Malachi mentions the tithe. The Old Testament Jews gave at least 23 percent, and the New Testament simply tells us to give regularly and with a cheerful heart (see 2 Corinthians 8–9). As you think about how much you can give, as well as how much you would *like* to give in the future, consider God's promise: *"The generous man will be prosperous, and he who waters will himself be watered"* (Proverbs 11:25).

Setting goals for giving (and deciding, in advance, how much money you will give) has a number of advantages over the sporadic and unplanned giving so prevalent among churchgoers today. For one thing, setting giving goals helps you refrain from impulsive or emotional overreaction (which can be a poor way to manage your God-given resources). Moreover, unless you *plan* to give, there's a good chance that you won't have any money left over once you've met your living expenses and savings goals. And, finally, taking a purposeful approach to giving offers you and your spouse the opportunity to look at the effectiveness of various ministries and give to the churches and organizations that can get the job done.

How much you can ultimately give depends, in large part, on how successful you are at setting and maintaining limits on your lifestyle. Judy and I have a system that works well for us. We are committed to giving a regular portion of our income to God's work, and that amount comes right off the top of our income. Then, since we know how much money we need to live on each month, we set that amount aside as "living income." Sometimes we have specific needs—such as when we decided to help pay for our daughter's graduate schooling, which increased our regular expenses. Apart from those things, however, our goal is to give above and beyond our living income to various ministries.

What are your passions? Is there a church, a missionary, or an outreach program you would like to support financially? Even without the potential impact of Y2K, the economic downturn that must surely come in the new millennium will offer unparalleled opportunities to care for the needy and proclaim God's love. If you prayerfully establish your giving goals now and make generosity a top priority in your budget, you will be ready to participate in God's exciting work as His purposes unfold.

Use a giving diary to write down your giving goals. Record how much you currently give (if you're not sure, check your old tax returns or checkbook registers), and establish a dollar amount or income percentage that you would like to give in the future. If you include a timeline or giving schedule in your goal, it will help you stay focused and track your progress. You also might want to set a secondary goal (you can call it your "faith goal") by deciding how much you will give if God provides you with more money in the future than you expect to earn or receive.

I'll leave you with one last thought. Planning is necessary and it is biblical, but don't lose the spontaneity that comes with serving God. If God reveals a need, even though you have given your planned amount, give anyway. That's where the joy can be found. *"Give, and it will be given to you; good measure, pressed down, shaken together, running over, they will pour into your lap. For by your standard of measure it will be measured to you in return"* (Luke 6:38).

---

1. *barna.org/pressnorevival.htm*

9

Principle Two:
Establish Long-Range Goals

In the last chapter, we saw that the primary purpose of money is to glorify and honor the Lord. Money is not an end in and of itself; rather, it is a tool we can use to accomplish our goals. It should go without saying that, for Christians, the goals we pursue ought to line up with God's purposes for our lives.

The goals we examined in the last chapter—lifestyle goals, debt reduction, savings, and giving—were shorter term in nature. In this chapter we will consider three longer-term objectives that can be accomplished through strategic investing: funding college educations, saving for retirement, and planning the distribution of an inheritance. As with the goals we've already considered, the overarching premise in this section is to structure your investments according to God's Word: *"Honor the Lord from your wealth, and from the first of all your produce"* (Proverbs 3:9).

Long-Term Goal #1: Meeting Education Costs

If you have children, funding their college educations is apt to be one of your larger financial needs and one of the main reasons why you need to invest. My children are grown, but as a grandparent I want to set money aside to help educate my grandchildren—especially my daughter's son, who has lived with us since he was two years old.

I may be a grandparent, but the financial challenges I face in saving for my grandson's education are no different than they would be if he were my own son. I calculate that it would cost about $50,000 to put my grandson through college if he started tomorrow. If I had the $50,000 in cash, I would only need a risk-free haven where I could "park" the money and keep pace with the inflating costs of a college education (currently about 5 or 6 percent per year).

Since I only have a portion of the money, I need another plan. I need growth, so I have to take a fairly aggressive approach to investing, assuming risk that I would not recommend for other goals, such as retirement income. So, I buy quality, high-growth companies and look for a return of about 20 percent per year, investing through a custodial account I have established in my grandson's name. I chose to use a custodial account because it allows me total control over the investments.

I have at least eight years before my grandson will need to access this college fund and, as I've said previously, I believe that good companies will ride out the coming recession and recover over the long run. If I had less time and more money, I might buy CDs and savings bonds as a means of protecting the cash for the short term until it was needed.

As you establish your college-funding goal, start by identifying your time horizon. How long do you have before you need the money?

Next, figure out how much you will need. The general rule is that the average cost of a college education is going up about 5 to 6 percent per year. So if the current annual cost is $8,000 (low side), then a four-year education would cost $32,000. If you can put the $32,000 aside, earmarked for college, you would only need to earn the inflation rate (after taxes). Otherwise, you will need a higher return, based on how much you can set aside, or invest annually.

When you consider your available resources and map a strategy for making up any shortfall you have, you may be forced to move into some aggressive funds in order to generate the money you need. Once you've figured out how much you need and how long you have, talk with a qualified financial advisor about which stock funds are best suited to your individual needs.

If I were looking for mutual funds to accomplish my investing goals, I would check out the *Consumer Reports* magazine annual edition on mutual funds, pick my category (aggressive, growth, balanced), and trust their assessment. Keep the immutable principle in mind: The greater the return expected, the greater the risk assumed.

Long-Term Goal #2: Retirement Planning

In our society there are two extremes when it comes to retirement planning: We either put nothing aside for the future or we sock away massive amounts of money with little thought for *how much* we will actually need or *why* we are saving so much.

I certainly have nothing against saving for retirement, and the Bible speaks to the wisdom of planning ahead: *"Go to the ant, O sluggard, observe her ways and be wise, which, having no chief, officer or ruler, prepares her food in the summer, and gathers her provision in the harvest"* (Proverbs 6:6–8). Just as the ant gathers food in the summertime so it will have provisions in the winter months, it's only logical that we prepare for the time when our incomes will decline by storing extra money while we can.

Unfortunately, though, we have shifted the focus in retirement planning from *providing* for the future to *hoarding* for the days ahead. Where does the Bible say we have to pad our retirement accounts? Where, for that matter, does it say we should retire at all? Nowhere! Retirement is a relatively modern concept, and it's one that we made up to fit our own goals and objectives.

Our contemporary obsession with retirement savings is fueled, in large part, by the alluring combination of tax-deferred IRAs and the overall economic growth we have experienced since World War II. What could be better than lowering your tax bill while you watch your nest egg grow? It's a tempting offer, but there is a downside. All too often our love affair with our retirement account comes at the expense of our current needs or our ability to give generously to God's work. We are robbing our families, and God, in a misguided attempt to build our own fortresses for the future.

I see this pattern played out on our radio program all the time. I have already noted how so many of today's average- and middle-income families maximize their stock market contributions and use credit cards to meet their living expenses. They may not realize what they are doing, but they're borrowing to invest.

A related problem crops up in the working-mother lifestyle many families have adopted today. A caller I talked with on the radio recently is typical of many of the stories I hear. This woman wanted to stay home with her two young children, but she felt that her family could not afford to live on her husband's salary alone.

"How much," I asked her, "are you putting into retirement savings each year?"

"Oh ,we save as much as we can," she proudly told me. "Last year, I think we put about $15,000 into our 401(k) accounts."

"And how much money do you and your husband make?"

"His salary is $50,000 and I make about $20,000."

I did some quick math and told her what I thought: She was working, in essence, to fund their retirement, and sacrificing her family's immediate needs and desires to do it. I told her what I believe: She'll have plenty of chances to work and make money. She'll only have one chance to raise her children.

For this woman, as for all of us, the key question to consider is "Why are we putting money aside for retirement?" I know of one couple who decided to put their two young sons in day care and "knock themselves out" in their jobs for the next 20 years so that they can retire and relax at age 50. Will the sacrifices they are making now be worth it? What will they do in their golden years?

Perhaps they will wind up like the couple Judy met on a cruise not long ago. They had been on 184 cruises since they retired! One hundred and eighty-four cruises! Is that a productive life for God's people? More importantly, is that a lifestyle that justifies abandoning all other worthwhile goals?

I don't think so. But then, I am not the one that you or anyone else will have to answer to on Judgment Day. I realize that most of you who are reading this book are looking forward to retirement. That's fine, but as you think about why you want to retire and how you plan to reach your goal, consider this message: *"Better is a little with the fear of the Lord, than great treasure and turmoil with it"* (Proverbs 15:16).

Personally, I don't plan to retire. I may not be able to do what I'm doing as I age, but I want to write or teach or speak for as long as I can. With that in mind, I am not looking to my retirement account to provide 100 percent of my income. I have saved enough money so that Judy will be taken care of if I die but, beyond that, it's going to help expand the Kingdom.

I love to play golf, but fortunately God has given me a golf limiter/regulator. Since I had my left shoulder blade removed, I can play no more than once per week. If God restores my scapula, then I'll believe He wants me to play more often. Of course, I'm being facetious. We have a very short time on this earth, and a very long time in eternity. My retirement will come in eternity. I trust yours will too. Foremost in your retirement planning, then, should be the prospect of standing before the Lord to give an account for the way you have handled your life and your money.

But, if you plan to slow down, you will need to decide where you'll invest your retirement dollars. With a traditional retirement account like an IRA, any money you invest is tax deferred, meaning that you don't have to pay taxes on your contributions until you withdraw the money (by which time you will likely be in a lower tax bracket and will therefore have to pay less).

Although traditional IRAs have long been the staple of retirement planning, many people (especially younger investors) are looking to Roth IRAs for their future financial security. With a Roth IRA, you pay taxes on your money *before* you invest it. Then it accumulates tax-free and you never have to pay taxes on it, even when the funds are withdrawn from the account at retirement age. For younger people with many years to accumulate earnings in a retirement account, the Roth IRA is an excellent investment tool. (Note: See your investment advisor for the rules and limitations of a Roth IRA.)

In addition to deciding *where* to invest your money, you need to carefully consider *how* you will make the transition from work to retirement. If all sources of retirement funds (including Social Security) generate less income than you are living on prior to retirement, you need to adjust your expenses—before you quit working.

Retirement can actually be more expensive—especially if it includes things like travel, golf, or other recreational activities. If you're not prepared to absorb these costs, you could find yourself having to reenter the workforce—probably in a lower-paying job than the one you left. If the numbers don't add up, you would be better off postponing retirement until you have developed an "exit strategy" that will work. It doesn't get easier after you quit working.

Obviously, there is much more to retirement planning than what we have covered here. I encourage you to talk with your spouse about your common goals for retirement and outline them in a durable diary so you can refer to them from time to time. You may think that's corny, but I'll guarantee that writing your goals is a discipline that does help to keep you on track.

When do you want to retire?

What do you see yourself doing after you leave your job?

How much money will you need to live on when you retire?

What percentage of that amount will your private retirement account need to provide?

Can you realistically achieve your goals?

Long-Term Goal #3: Inheritance Issues

The final goal-setting area I want to cover is the distribution of your estate. Why am I including this long-term planning in a book about the new millennium, which is already on our doorstep? Two reasons.

First, estate planning is a vital part of any sound financial strategy, and if you want to invest effectively in the years ahead, you must plot your course with the big picture in mind. If you know, for instance, that you want to use the proceeds from your estate to create a trust on behalf of a favorite charity, you might choose a different investment strategy than you would if your main objective was to provide for the raising and educating of your young children.

For instance, I recently counseled a widow who owned a large land tract that a local church wanted. Rather than just sell the church the land, pay the taxes, and invest the proceeds, she decided to set up a charitable trust with the land. The trust provides her with a lifetime income, a current tax deduction, and avoids all taxes on the land sale. When she dies, the church will own the land outright. To achieve the same investment return, she would have needed a guaranteed return of nearly 25 percent on the net sale proceeds! She wins, the church wins, and the Lord's work advances.

How and where you choose to distribute your assets could well be affected by whatever happens in the economy in the next few years. You may be planning, like so many people, to simply leave an inheritance to your children in your will, for distribution after your death. But, if a recession leaves your children in a precarious financial position, you may want to give them some money before then.

One financial advisor I know is convinced that the stock market will crash in the near future. Rather than leave his children's inheritance in the market, he has converted his holdings into U.S. government securities and cash. And although he is only 60 years old, he and his wife have begun to reduce the size of their estate through an aggressive gifting program, giving the maximum allowable $10,000 per year to each of their children and to a number of Christian organizations.

Transferring wealth to your children while you are still living is hardly a new concept. In fact, giving while you're living is more biblical than giving after death. Scripture is filled with illustrations of families for whom lifetime giving was the norm. The Bible tells us that *"Now Abraham gave all that he had to Isaac; but to the sons of his concubines, Abraham gave gifts while he was still living, and sent them away from his son Isaac eastward, to the land of the east"* (Genesis 25:5–6).

And in the New Testament, Jesus' parable of the prodigal son, in which a young man asks his father for his portion of the estate, would not have seemed odd at the time. Back then, it was not at all unusual for a father to set up his children in a home or in business while he was still around to act as a mentor and confidant.

Today, this practice has some definite advantages. In addition to the opportunity lifetime giving affords for helping your children learn to manage money wisely, there are some very favorable tax consequences associated with using the annual gift exclusion to reduce the size (and taxability) of your estate. Under this provision, you and your spouse are allowed to give up to $10,000 per year each, to as many individuals as you like.

Another benefit of lifetime giving comes with charitable giving. Again, the tax advantages of using charitable contributions to reduce the size of your estate and save taxes currently make this a wise strategy. Plus, you have the added reward of being able to see your dollars at work for God's kingdom here on earth.

If such a gifting program appeals to you, consider establishing a charitable remainder trust. Let's say, for example, that you were shrewd enough to have bought Microsoft, America Online, Amazon.com, and other technological success stories early on and that your portfolio has quadrupled in size. If you sold the stocks you would lose a hefty chunk of your asset value to capital gains taxes.

If, however, you transferred the stock to a charitable remainder trust, you would avoid these taxes (as well as the eventual estate taxes), and you'd have the added benefit of a current charitable deduction to use on your tax return. And the charity could sell the appreciated securities without paying any capital gains tax.

But that's not all. When you put the assets into a trust, you reap an annual income distribution equal to an agreed-upon percentage of the trust's total value. In other words, you can reduce taxes, benefit your favorite charity, and generate a lifetime income stream for yourself that could easily exceed the amount you would receive from earnings if you had held onto the stock!

Charitable remainder trusts are just one of many estate planning tools you can use to meet your inheritance objectives. For more information on these and other tools and strategies, please consult your financial advisor.

At this point, I want to challenge you to think through your estate plan and establish three primary goals. First, decide how much money you want to give to your children. Don't simply assume that you must give an equal amount to each one of your heirs. Some of your children may be better equipped to handle money wisely than others, and some may have specific needs (special medical care) that might warrant giving them a larger portion of the estate.

The size or equality of an inheritance should not be a determining factor in whether or not your children feel loved; that security, if it is genuine, should be established well before you die. After all, the Lord does not deal equally with each of us when it comes to financial blessings. Does the fact that I have less, materially, than my friend with the fancy California home mean that I feel less loved by God? Of course not!

Next, decide how much money you want to leave to charity and which charities you want to support. If you are not very familiar with an organization's financial structure, ask to see a copy of its latest annual report (IRS Form 990). And to ensure that your money is used effectively, look at factors such as the group's leadership (are godly people in charge?) and their track record (are they getting results for the kingdom?). Since you are leaving estate assets that may not be distributed for years, you need to be sure the organizations have good long-term plans, including leadership-succession plans.

Third, decide how and when you want the inheritance to be distributed.

Record your three main goals. Take this information (as well as the other goals you have established in this chapter) with you when you meet with the attorney or financial advisor who will help you craft your will.

Inheritance Goals
1. How much money do we want to leave to our children?
2. How much money do we want to leave to charity?
3. How and when do we want to distribute this inheritance?

Establish Long-Range Goals

At this point, you should have a clearer idea of where you want to go or what you want to accomplish in terms of your lifestyle, debt load, savings plan, giving goals, college funding, retirement, and estate distribution. With these goals in mind, and with an understanding of what is likely to happen in the overall economy, you can develop an investment strategy to carry you well into the new millennium.

How you pursue each of your goals will depend, in part, on your individual temperament and your personal tolerance for risk—issues that we will cover in the next chapter. And again, as you make your investment decisions, remember to check your motivation against your short- and long-term goals. Are you actively seeking to honor the Lord with your wealth? Do you have a vision for how and where God wants you to use your money? Do you know why you are investing?

"For to a person who is good in His sight He has given wisdom and knowledge and joy, while to the sinner He has given the task of gathering and collecting so that He may give to one who is good in God's sight. This too is vanity and striving after wind" (Ecclesiastes 2:26).

Principle Three:
How Much Risk You Can Take

Single or married, how you determine your risk threshold is vitally important to the success of your investment strategy. For married couples, reaching a consensus takes on added importance when you consider that the majority of women outlive their husbands.

Men, if you were to die today, would your wife feel comfortable with the way your assets are allocated? Would she follow your financial plan, or would she bail out of your investment portfolio, even if it meant taking a loss? Do not underestimate the importance of unity as you make your investment choices. Not only will a consensus promote harmony in your marriage, it could be a deciding factor in whether a surviving spouse will continue the current plan.

Let me assure you that the surviving spouse will ultimately choose his or her own comfort level. If the wife has not been consulted about the investment plan and decides to make changes, she may be duped by some emotional sales program.

On a more immediate level, the pertinent questions would be, "Do you know how much money you could afford to lose?" "If the market dropped precipitously, at what point would you decide to bail out?" "Would you feel more comfortable sitting out the market for a few months immediately before and after the Y2K event, or are you comfortable riding out any downturns?" Your answers to questions like these will help shape your investment strategy for the new millennium.

Often, how much risk you and your spouse can handle depends on two relatively objective factors: your *ages* and your *temperaments* or personality styles. Obviously, your age is easy to pinpoint. Even though your individual temperament may be more complex, it also can be assessed within certain parameters. First, let's look at a typical scenario that involves a husband and wife who disagree about their financial planning strategy. We'll see how personality issues figure into their approach.

Hearing Each Other

Steve glanced up, then looked down again, his frustration evident. Next to him sat his wife Leslie. Studying her hands, she looked up only occasionally, and only (it seemed to me) to check my reaction to her husband's comments.

Recently, Steve and Leslie had inherited some stock worth about $150,000 that had belonged to Leslie's grandfather; he had accumulated it by investing in blue-chip companies. Now Steve was prepared to sell the stock and use the proceeds to invest in several hightech companies. "The way I see it," he said, "those companies are where the *real* money is. I don't want to seem greedy, but if we're going to pay for our kids' college educations, we're going to need to look at some more aggressive investments."

Leslie was far more cautious. The blue chips had served her grandfather well, and she didn't want to gamble with her inheritance. "Isn't there some way to invest without assuming so much risk?" she asked anxiously.

Steve and Leslie are fairly typical of many couples I meet. They tend to be opposites. If one is paralyzed by the fear of loss, the other is engaged in wildly speculative investing. This is a generalization, I know, but it is more often right than wrong.

Different Paradigms

Many speculators get irritated when their spouses don't agree with their investment plans. Steve complained about Leslie's attitude. "Where is the trust my wife is supposed to have in me?" His words were angry and pointed. Leslie got the message. Like many conservatives, Leslie's defense was simply to withdraw and make no decisions.

It's important to understand why a spouse makes the decisions he or she does. Usually it's not a desire to hurt the other person; rather, it's a desire to defend his or her own insecurities. All too often both spouses can pursue what they perceive to be the best for their family and miss the mark completely. In Steve's case his ego was hurt.

Andrew was a construction company owner. He thought his wife Sheila should have been pleased with their upward mobility as he moved them from house to house *five* times in the first three years of their marriage. He built their first house, moved in, and immediately put a "For Sale" sign in the front yard. He then began building a second, more upscale "spec" home. The first house sold before he had completed the second, so they moved into an apartment. As soon as he could complete construction, they moved into the second house and started the process all over again. Between their third and fourth moves, Sheila got pregnant with their second child.

Of course, two babies in diapers complicated Andrew's agenda for prosperity. His wife was more concerned with stability; she resented not being able to decorate the nursery because it might not suit the tastes of a prospective buyer. The combination of Andrew's and Sheila's financial goals and insecurities placed a tremendous strain on their marriage.

- Andrew defended his position well. He said he couldn't understand why she didn't see that he was "doing it all *for* her."
- Sheila countered that she couldn't understand why he didn't see that he was "doing all of it *to* her."
- To him, their moves were business; he was *selling houses*.
- To her, their moves were personal; she was *leaving homes*.

It's not surprising that their very different perspectives drove a wedge between them that threatened to destroy their marriage.

Different Perspectives

In financial matters, more often than not husbands expect their wives to follow dutifully as they steer through the market, exercising their personal investment strategies. Many wives would be willing to settle for less return sometimes, in exchange for less stress. The more each person insists on his or her own way, the deeper the wedge is driven.

The ancestral heritage of men is to be hunters. Men are drawn easily to "the kill": to achieve and conquer. Steve wanted to put their newfound riches into growth stocks that would "pay off big" (assuming they paid off at all). The prospect of quick riches blinded him to the risk of losing something far more important: Leslie's confidence and trust.

I recall what a family counselor once said, "Men hate waiting while their wives shop for clothes and trinkets; women hate waiting (often for much of their lives) while their husbands shop for fame and glory." Steve and Leslie are two very different people. If they could work together, their differences would make them better.

One of the problems any couple faces in communicating is obvious: women and men don't even look at each other the same way, literally! A university study revealed that young girls prefer to sit facing each other, so they can be close and make lots of eye contact as they talk. However, most boys seem to prefer less close contact. Adult men tend to communicate less directly, even with their close friends. They sit next to each other in the car, at the ball game, or in the fishing boat, but their conversation seems to bounce off nearby surfaces rather than being close and personal.

It has been my observation that most men tend to tell their wives about the investment strategies in the vaguest of terms, rather than to involve them in the process. Most investment salespeople agree that it is far easier to sell investments to men (in general) than to most women. Why? Women want to talk, think, and pray about it. Men just want to get it done!

Different Pace and Priority

In addition to our gender differences, there is also the matter of differences in our personality style's behavioral traits. In marriage, opposite traits often attract, as if we are trying to find our "missing half."

I have found that the four-factor personality evaluation is very helpful in enabling couples to see how and why they respond to situations in life. Later in this chapter there is a personality style assessment for husbands and wives. It does not focus on differences between genders; rather, it reveals differences in personalities as husbands and wives interact on a variety of issues. I want to help you understand a few basics about your personality.

First of all, many behavioral scientists have identified *four* basic personality styles into which most human beings can be classified. In the following illustration, you can see that the divisions come in two areas: your *pace* and your *priority*.[1]

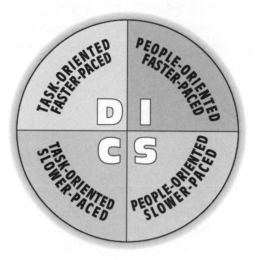

- The *pace* of a **D**-type (Dominant) personality style is faster. The *priority* is accomplishing tasks.
- The *pace* of an **I**-type (Influencer) personality style is also faster, but the *priority* involves associating with people.
- The *pace* of an **S**-type (Supporter) personality style is slower, and the *priority* involves helping people.
- The *pace* of a **C**-type (Compliant/perfectionist) personality style is slower, but the *priority* involves doing things correctly.

You also can think of these personality style differences in terms of a *motor* and a *compass:* Your "motor" is the speed at which you tend to go through life—faster or slower. Your "compass" is the direction in which you feel pulled—toward tasks or toward people.

It's easy to see how these differences in *pace* and *priority* can lead to conflicting values, even in the middle of a committed and loving relationship. This is because each of the four styles has different needs and expresses them in different ways.

- **D**-types tend to be driven by results. They are ambitious and want to get ahead. (Often wrong, but never in doubt.)
- **I**-types are more motivated by interaction and social recognition. They are emotion-based in their response to people and events. (Everything they have ever done is hanging on a wall someplace.)
- **S**-types like stability and resist unplanned changes in their routine. Predictable is a good word to describe them. (They get the job done.)
- **C**-types are concerned about accuracy and want things to be done correctly. Their high standards of performance motivate them to perfection rather than to excellence. Their response to life tends to be conservative. (They stop at red lights, even at 2:00 A.M., when there's no traffic.)

Different Procedures

In relation to money, I thought back on my experiences in trying to help various personality types budget their money. As you gain an understanding of the forces that propel different personality types, generally you can predict how they will respond to the limits imposed by a spending allowance:

- To **D**-type personalities, budgets are "guesstimates" of what they actually spend. They will barely glance at detailed expense summaries and prefer graphs. A home or family budget represents little more than a "target" for **D**-types.

- To **I**-type personalities, budgets are mysteries. They prefer flexibility, not limitations. The only reason they will stick to a budget is if there is a reward—or recognition.
- **S**-type individuals work hard to stay *under* budget. They are team players and feel uncomfortable making decisions on their own. They like to save for unplanned expenses; and, they don't like surprises!
- **C**-type individuals strive to live *within* budgets. They understand the details of income and expenses and have a tight control on costs. They love bargains and delight in cutting costs. They live to budget.

Of course, no one is purely just a **D** or just an **I**, **S**, or **C**. Individual styles are blends of all four types, to a greater or lesser degree, but usually one element tends to dominate the four basic personality traits.

In marriage, the differences in personality styles can create conflict. Initially, "opposites *attract.*" But eventually, opposites *attack!* However, this doesn't have to be true.

Differences can strengthen a marriage, if the differences are accepted as normal. When husbands and wives are able to listen to each other and cooperate in meeting each other's needs, the differing viewpoints of a husband-wife team contribute to a balanced life together. They learn how to *complete,* rather than *compete!*

The Way We Handle Risk

It's been said that men can't understand life until they *do* it, and women can't understand life until they *tell* somebody about it.

When you add in *age, gender,* and *personality* differences, it's not surprising that each of us has an individual comfort level about making financial decisions, especially in our complex society. Understanding your composite tolerance for risk is a key pre-requisite to good investing. Therefore, you also need to know how much risk your spouse is willing and able to accept, as well as your own. If there is a significant gap between the two of you, you need to stop and resolve it!

Different Processes

Personality styles not only influence how we tolerate risk; they also influence the ways we communicate with each other.

While working on this book one evening, I was sitting in our den watching a news program, chatting with my 10-year-old grandson, and discussing an investment idea with my wife Judy. I had no difficulty with that scenario; after all, we high Ds usually have several things going at one time.

Judy got up to leave and I asked her, "What's the problem?"

She replied, "I can't talk to someone who won't look at me."

I didn't say so, but I thought, *How can I look at her and still write, watch TV, and check out Ryan's new model too?* Then I got the point. I couldn't.

Even though I teach, sometimes I forget that we process infor-mation differently. When we go walking in our neighborhood, Judy will comment on the houses and the lake. I don't even notice that there are houses or a lake. I'm concentrating on my goal: walking. The same general rule applies across the board with contrasting personalities.

The simple personality assessments in this chapter are for husbands and wives to use. If you understand the helpmate God has provided, it will greatly enhance your communications. The second assessment looks at your *risk tolerance* in relation to investing. Hopefully, this will help you design a plan that will be financially sound, while allowing both of you to sleep at night.

The Four Dimensions of DISC

D

DOMINANT: People who have a high level of dominance (High D) are naturally motivated to control the home environment. They are usually assertive, direct, and strong willed. They are typically bold and not afraid to take strong action to get the desired results. They function best in a challenging environment.

Examples:
Paul	General George Patton
Sarah	Barbara Walters

I

INFLUENCING: People who are highly influencing (High I) are driven naturally to relate to others. Usually they are verbal, friendly, outgoing, and optimistic. They are typically enthusiastic motivators and will seek out others to help them accomplish results. They function best in a friendly environment.

Examples:
Peter	Ronald Reagan
Mary Magdalene	Kathie Lee Gifford

C

CONSCIENTIOUS: People who have a high level of conscientiousness (High C, also called cautiousness) are focused on doing things right. Usually they are detail oriented and find it easy to follow prescribed guidelines. Typically they strive for accuracy and quality and, therefore, set high standards for themselves and for others. They function best in a structured environment.

Examples:
Elijah	Albert Einstein
Luke	General Omar Bradley

S

STEADY: People who have a high level of steadiness (High S) are naturally motivated to cooperate with and support others. They are usually patient, consistent, and very dependable. Being pleasant and easygoing makes them excellent team players. They function best in a supportive, harmonious environment.

Examples:
Abraham	President George Bush
Hannah	Mother Teresa

Continue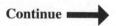

How Much Risk You Can Take

Survey A

DIRECTIONS

FOCUS: The focus for this survey is **your typical behavior.** Respond based on **how you most naturally behave.**

RESPOND: Rate each line of words from left to right on a 4, 3, 2, 1 scale with **4 being the word that best describes your naturally motivated behavior and 1 being the word that is least like you.** *Use all ratings (4, 3, 2, 1) in each line and use each rating only once.* To change a response, mark through it and write the new response to the left of the box. Study the example below before starting.

Correct Example A: → $\boxed{4}$ Enthusiastic $\boxed{1}$ Loyal $\boxed{2}$ Detailed $\boxed{3}$ Commanding

Incorrect Example B: → $\boxed{4}$ Enthusiastic $\boxed{1}$ Loyal $\boxed{3}$ Detailed $\boxed{4}$ Commanding

Incorrect: Use each rating only once as in Example A.

4 is most like you ← 4   3   2   1 → 1 is least like you

	I		II		III		IV
→	Commanding		Enthusiastic		Loyal		Detailed
→	Decisive		Expressive		Lenient		Particular
→	Tough-Minded		Convincing		Kind		Meticulous
→	Independent		Fun Loving		Peaceful		Follow Rules
→	Daring		People-Oriented		Understanding		High Standards
→	Dominant		Lively		Charitable		Serious
→	Courageous		Cheerful		Merciful		Precise
→	Confident		Inspiring		Supportive		Logical
→	Fearless		Good Mixer		Patient		Conscientious
→	Non-Conforming		Talkative		Gentle		Analytical
→	Assertive		Popular		Even-Paced		Organized
→	Take-Charge		Uninhibited		Good Listener		Factual
→	Aggressive		Vibrant		Cooperative		Accurate
→	Direct		Excitable		Gracious		Efficient
→	Frank		Influencing		Accommodating		Focused
→	Forceful		Animated		Agreeable		Systematic

Total ☐   Total ☐   Total ☐   Total ☐

Add the numbers in each column ➡

Survey B

DIRECTIONS

FOCUS: The focus for this survey is **your typical behavior.** Respond based on **how you most naturally behave.**

RESPOND: Rate each line of words from left to right on a 4, 3, 2, 1 scale with **4 being the word that best describes your naturally motivated behavior and 1 being the word that is least like you.** *Use all ratings (4, 3, 2, 1) in each line and use each rating only once.* To change a response, mark through it and write the new response to the left of the box. Study the example below before starting.

Correct Example A: → `4` Enthusiastic `1` Loyal `2` Detailed `3` Commanding

Incorrect Example B: → `4` Enthusiastic `1` Loyal `3` Detailed `4` Commanding

Incorrect: Use each rating only once as in Example A.

4 is most like you ← 4 3 2 1 → 1 is least like you

I	II	III	IV
Commanding	Enthusiastic	Loyal	Detailed
Decisive	Expressive	Lenient	Particular
Tough-Minded	Convincing	Kind	Meticulous
Independent	Fun-Loving	Peaceful	Follow Rules
Daring	People-Oriented	Understanding	High Standards
Dominant	Lively	Charitable	Serious
Courageous	Cheerful	Merciful	Precise
Confident	Inspiring	Supportive	Logical
Fearless	Good Mixer	Patient	Conscientious
Non-Conforming	Talkative	Gentle	Analytical
Assertive	Popular	Even-Paced	Organized
Take-Charge	Uninhibited	Good Listener	Factual
Aggressive	Vibrant	Cooperative	Accurate
Direct	Excitable	Gracious	Efficient
Frank	Influencing	Accommodating	Focused
Forceful	Animated	Agreeable	Systematic

Total ☐   Total ☐   Total ☐   Total ☐

Add the numbers in each column

Personality Profiles

How to Score

1. Add the (top to bottom) numbers in each column and plot the results from Surveys A and B as shown in this example.

2. Note that the sample graph has a High S profile.

3. Identify the high points (those above the midline) and then read "The Four Dimensions of DISC" to learn what the high points represent.

EXAMPLE

SURVEY A TOTALS

TOTAL I ____45____ = D
TOTAL II ____31____ = I
TOTAL III ____51____ = S
TOTAL IV ____33____ = C
TOTAL MUST = 160

SURVEY B TOTALS

TOTAL I ____22____ = D
TOTAL II ____32____ = I
TOTAL III ____54____ = S
TOTAL IV ____52____ = C
TOTAL MUST = 160

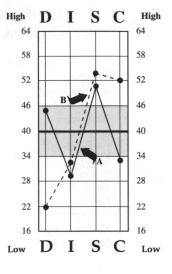

Plot the A and B Profiles

1. Using the totals from Survey A and B, plot the two DISC dimensions on the graph to the right. The result will be your natural personality profiles.

2. Use a solid line for Survey A and a dashed line (or colored pencil) for Survey B.

3. Identify the high points (those above the midline) and then read "The Four Dimensions of DISC" to learn what the high points represent.

SURVEY A TOTALS

TOTAL I ____ = D
TOTAL II ____ = I
TOTAL III ____ = S
TOTAL IV ____ = C

SURVEY B TOTALS

TOTAL I ____ = D
TOTAL II ____ = I
TOTAL III ____ = S
TOTAL IV ____ = C

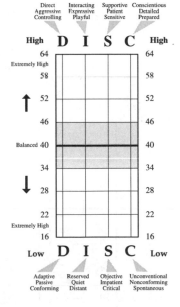

RISK TOLERANCE SURVEY
Now complete this additional inventory for Persons A and B

Inventory A		**Inventory B**	
Rate the following words from 1 to 4, where 1 is LEAST like you, and 4 is MOST like you.*		Rate the following words from 1 to 4, where 1 is LEAST like you, and 4 is MOST like you.*	
Adventurous	____	Adventurous	____
Ambitious	____	Ambitious	____
Courageous	____	Courageous	____
Daring	____	Daring	____
Fearless	____	Fearless	____
Gutsy	____	Gutsy	____
Opportunistic	____	Opportunistic	____
Pioneering	____	Pioneering	____
Risk-Taker	____	Risk-Taker	____
Venturesome	____	Venturesome	____
Add your scores	[ ]	**Add your scores**	[ ]

*Take this assessment in regard to your <u>financial</u> attitudes.

Plot the totals from the inventory for A and B on the Risk Scales below

RISK SCALE

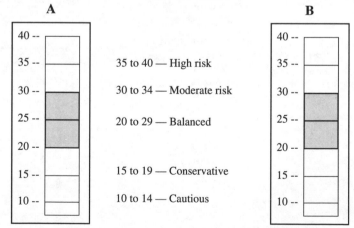

A

40 --	
35 --	35 to 40 — High risk
30 --	30 to 34 — Moderate risk
25 --	20 to 29 — Balanced
20 --	
15 --	15 to 19 — Conservative
10 --	10 to 14 — Cautious

B

40 --
35 --
30 --
25 --
20 --
15 --
10 --

How Much Risk You Can Take

Assuming that you and your spouse have completed both the personality assessment and the risk assessment, you should have a reasonable idea of why you approach financial issues differently. Now what you want to do is resolve the differences. If you find that either of you scored below the centerline in risk, it means that you need to be sensitive to that. It does not mean to eliminate all possible risks from your investment portfolio.

In the first place, that is virtually impossible. In the second place, it would be poor stewardship. Reasonable risk is the answer, along with good communications.

If the husband is a "high **D**," with a high tolerance for risk taking, and the wife is a "high **S**," with a low tolerance for risk, then investing in eBay.com, Priceline.com, and Amazon.com probably won't give you much peace in the home. But perhaps a compromise will work. Set aside 10 percent of the assets for high-growth investing—but no more!

Most of the high-tech, risk-prone stocks won't collapse, even if prices fall 50 percent. So the most exposure you would have is a 5 percent potential loss. Most low risk takers can accept that scenario if they understand that it is the *maximum* potential loss. What they can't handle is the double-or-nothing mentality that seems to pervade our society today.

Know Thyself

The personality survey can be a very good tool in developing good communications. When I first took it, I was startled to see how accurately it assessed my strengths and weaknesses. I also was surprised to see not only how different Judy and I are (I already knew that) but why we are so different: We approach problems from a totally different perspective.

I am a **D-C** personality.
My pattern looks like this:

Judy is an **S-C** personality.
Her pattern looks like this:

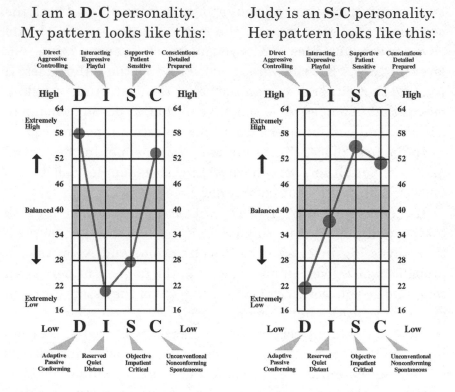

I tend to not listen well and to make quick decisions. I also tend to see all the errors that others make (my perfectionism). I like clear, concise facts and two-minute phone conversations.

Judy, on the other hand, likes long discussions, empathy, plenty of time to look, and several people with whom she can discuss a decision.

See the problem?

Individually, our investment strategies would be very different, as would the amount of counsel we would seek (or take). That does not mean my wife's financial decisions would be worse than mine—only different. Together we make better decisions than either of us does separately.

Not only do we look at investments differently, we look at different kinds of investments. Since Judy is more of a "tangible" person, she leans toward real estate investing. Since I look at property as work, I lean toward stocks, bonds, and mutual funds. The mix has consistently helped us to maintain a good balance.

I have known only a handful of married couples who are more similar than different. And in most cases, compromise and agreement are often reached too soon. By this I mean that since they lack different personality perspectives they would benefit from listening to other viewpoints before making their decisions.

For instance, if both the husband and wife are risk takers, they should discuss their strategy with a qualified individual who tends to be more cautious when investing. And if both the husband and wife are very conservative in their approach, they should discuss their strategies with someone who tends to be a more aggressive investor. I am not saying to follow someone else's advice blindly, but they do need to hear some ideas other than their own.

Tips for Good Communications

In discussing financial matters, the following suggestions are helpful, once you know and appreciate your spouse's personality traits.

When talking with a **D-type** personality, it helps to
- be targeted in getting to the main point.
- be brief and credible.
- focus on overcoming obstacles.
- use logic, rather than emotions.
- provide choices.

When talking with **I-type** personalities, it helps to
- help them turn talk into action.
- focus on what they have achieved so far.
- let them express their thoughts and ideas without attack.
- set short-term goals with incentives along the way.
- provide examples of how your plan has worked for others.

When talking with **S-type** personalities, it helps to
- be calm and nonthreatening.
- allow them time to adjust to change.
- show how they (and others) will benefit.
- set aside an unhurried time for discussion.
- provide reassurance as they continue to raise doubts.

When talking with a **C-type** personality, it helps to
- list the "pro" and "con" arguments.
- supply details and think through your responses.
- listen and answer thoughtfully.
- agree with the person when he or she is right.
- provide clear and accurate information.

Not How Much Risk Can You Handle, But How Much Should You Handle?

The majority of people who jumped out of buildings during the 1929 stock market crash would have made their money back within 15 years, if they had stayed the course. But investing in a volatile climate takes nerve, and not many investors have the nerves to withstand a large drop in the value of their portfolios, including the risk takers.

In light of the financial instability that will likely mark the new millennium in its infancy, it is entirely possible that nervous investors will send the market into a spiral. If you are caught in this spiral, you'll need to focus on the long term. I'll guarantee you that the very same people who scoff at negative forecasts are the very ones who will express alarm, if and when the economy turns down. Just as you have to weigh their counsel now, you will need to weigh it then also. Things are never as good as they believe—nor are they as bad.

Of course, as I said before, deciding whether to hold on or to sell out doesn't have to be an either/or choice. You might choose to leave a reasonable portion of your portfolio in stocks and hold the balance in cash, government securities, or other very secure investments.

The Fine Art of Compromise

So what portfolio mix is right for you? That's totally up to you and your spouse. Work out an arrangement that satisfies both of you. If you're unable to agree, seek competent outside help from a Christian financial advisor who has the experience you lack. As one very successful businessman says, "A person with experience is never at the mercy of someone with a theory."[2]

One Last Tip for Similar Couples

In my experience, the few similar couples I have known were mostly "high S" personalities. (Research shows that S-type traits are strongest in more than a third of the population.)

For example, one couple I knew both had "high S" personalities. I always chuckled when we went out to lunch with them. He would ask, "Honey, where would you like to eat?"

She would reply, "Oh, Sweetheart, I really don't care; anywhere you want to go is fine with me."

Then he would say, "No, dear. You choose." And they would go back and forth, as nice as you please, without ever making a decision! Faced with the possibility of starvation, I would eventually jump in and choose the restaurant for all of us—much to their obvious relief. They would rather go along with someone else's decision than to have to make one.

For S-type personalities, having a financial planner or advisor can be very helpful in mapping out financial strategies and making tough choices. Of course, you (and not your financial advisor) must shoulder the ultimate responsibility for deciding where to invest your money. And the better you know yourself—your personality, age requirements, and tolerance for risk—the better equipped you will be, not only to make wise investment choices but also to choose and work with a financial advisor. Remember, if he or she gives you bad advice, he or she will be sorry. But you'll be broke!

———————

1. This concept of "pace" and "priority" is central to virtually all four-trait human behavior models. It was explained first by Dr. William Moulton Marston in his book, *The Emotions of Normal People*, published in 1928. Numerous books about personality styles have been written for Christians, including the following:
   * *Understand How Others Misunderstand You* (Moody Press)
   * *Your Child Wonderfully Made* (Moody Press)
   * *Who Do You Think You Are . . . Anyway?* Robert A. Rohm (Atlanta: Personality Insights, 1997)
   * *Different Children, Different Needs* (Questar)
   These books use the DISC language.

   Another model, using the classic temperaments of choleric, sanguine, phlegmatic, and melancholy, has been advanced in the following:
   * *Personality Plus: How to Understand Others by Understanding Yourself*, Florence Littauer (Ada, MI: Revell, 1994).
   * *Your Personality Tree*, Florence Littauer (Waco, TX: Word Publishing, 1989).
   * *Spirit-Controlled Temperament*, Tim LaHaye (Wheaton: Tyndale House, 1993).
2. Bill J. Bonstetter, et al., *DISC, the Universal Language, A Reference Manual* (Scottsdale: Target Training International, 1993).

Principle Four:
Seek Wise Counsel

Stuart and his brother-in-law Tom were on the roof when Stuart's cordless phone rang. "Hello?" he said, putting down his hammer.

Tom positioned the next piece of shingle as he listened to Stuart's end of the conversation.

"Uh-huh," Stuart said, and then paused to listen. "Really? That sounds pretty good."

Thinking that it must be a sales call, Tom held the shingles with one hand and made wrap-it-up motions with the other. After all, they were working 30 feet above the ground and he didn't want to prolong the job. Tom really liked his brother-in-law, and he was happy to help him reroof his house, but there were limits to how far he would go. And he could still feel the soreness from where Stuart had slipped off the ladder and landed on him yesterday. *Maybe,* Tom thought wryly, *we should have left the job to the professionals.*

Tom's ears perked up as he heard his brother-in-law's next words. "I don't know," Stuart said. "Two thousand dollars sounds pretty steep. But hold on, my brother-in-law is right here. I'll find out if he wants to go in with me.

"Want some stock?" Stuart asked enthusiastically.

"Are you kidding me?" Tom replied.

"Not a bit. It sounds like a great deal. It's a digital cellular phone company; this guy says they're setting the standard for new technology in the telecommunications industry."

"Do you know this guy?"

"Never heard of him before right now. But he sounds like he knows what he's talking about."

Tom was not convinced. "How much would we have to buy?"

"He recommends 100 shares. At $20 a share, we're only talking $2,000. And we could split it. So how 'bout it? This technology stuff is really hot, you know. I say we go for it."

"Well . . . okay. But don't say anything to the girls—at least not until we see which way it's going to go."

Tom listened as Stuart made the purchase. His brother-in-law appeared intent on whatever the stockbroker was saying. "Oh, really?" Stuart said, and then covered the mouthpiece. "He does financial planning too," he whispered. "Well yeah," he said, turning his attention back to the phone, "I guess we could use some professional advice."

Oh, great, Tom said to himself, smothering a smile. *Now he wants to hire a professional.*

Although Stuart and Tom eventually made a small profit on their transaction, what they did—buying stock in a company they knew nothing about from a broker they had never heard of—flies in the face of conventional and biblical wisdom. You might get away with it once, but that kind of investment advice usually will get you broke!

When it comes to effective investing, few things matter more than the soundness of the counsel you receive.

Educate Yourself First

Regardless of whether you plan to work with a stockbroker or another professional financial advisor, start by familiarizing yourself with various investment strategies, mutual funds, and other products. The Bible says, *"The beginning of wisdom is: acquire wisdom; and with all your acquiring, get understanding"* (Proverbs 4:7).

Hiring a professional advisor should not be the very first step in acquiring financial wisdom. In fact, it really could wind up costing you—maybe not all you have but a healthy sum, nonetheless. For the price of one month's counsel with a good planner, you could buy more investing magazines, books, and tapes than you could digest in a year.

Learn the ropes on your own time and at your own pace, instead of paying a counselor to walk you through the basics. Once you understand the basics, then seek the professional counsel you need. He or she will think you're a lot smarter, and you'll be better able to evaluate the advice you get.

The Appendix offers a more complete list of recommended reading, but I'll give you a few of my favorite picks to get you started. These are the resources I use to stay current with what's happening in the economy and in the investing world. I review magazines like *Money, Worth, Forbes,* and *Fortune,* and if a mutual fund pops up as a "buy" in more than one of these magazines, I consider that a favorable sign.

Two favorite books on my shelf are Austin Pryor's *Sound Mind Investing* (Moody Press, 1996) and Peter Lynch's *One up on Wall Street* (Viking Penguin, 1990). I like these books because they are easy to read and aimed at a very practical level. In other words, you can understand them and apply the advice. I also read a couple of newspapers pretty regularly, including *The Wall Street Journal; Investors Business Daily;* and, less frequently, *Morningstar,* which evaluates the performance of various mutual funds.

Of course, the Internet has put a whole new wealth of information at our fingertips. Whether I am at home or at the office, I can get much of the research I need by going to *www.compuserve.com, www.infoseek.com*, or *www.hotbot.com*. These are simple, easy-to-use search programs that, with a little practice, anyone can use easily. For stock market information, I like *www.cross-walk.com*, a Christian Internet company, and *www.pointcast.com*.

In short, you have to have some investment knowledge before you can understand your options. And the more you know, the better your decisions are apt to be.

Choosing a Professional Financial Advisor

Acting solely as your own financial advisor may be an economical way to invest, but it has its downsides. To do the job right, you have to have a certain level of expertise. Obviously, monitoring both the overall economy and your personal investments can take a lot of time. Using the reading list I just gave you, for example, could require several hours a month to keep current.

My recommendation, therefore, is that you soak up as much financial and investment information as you can—learning the "language," so to speak—and then find a professional financial counselor who understands both your goals and your tolerance for risk. But finding the right advisor can be time-consuming. You need someone you can trust and feel comfortable to ask questions. We all have had bad experiences with auto mechanics who treated every question like it was a threat. Typically, you don't ask very many questions after that. The same is true of your financial counselor. Finding the right match can be tough.

In 1995 I was diagnosed with a rare and difficult form of cancer that has virtually no traditional treatment, except surgery. So I began a search for the best specialist I could find. One of the lessons I learned when I was being treated for cancer is that you really can't "judge a book by its cover." Sitting in a doctor's office, I had no way of knowing whether that particular physician had been the valedictorian of his class or if he had graduated dead last. No one, after all, posts a sign that says, "I was last in my medical class. Don't take my advice."

It's much the same with financial counselors. Just because someone has a plush office or works with a big-name firm doesn't mean he or she is particularly talented at that job. It's up to you, the investor, to tell the difference between the good, the bad, and the mediocre.

The Compatibility Test

One of the first things to consider when choosing financial advisors is their investment style. Do their goals line up with yours? Is their risk tolerance on your level?

When I was doing the research for this book, I surveyed a dozen successful investment counselors, with reference to the strategies they used on behalf of their clients. They are regarded as leaders in the investment field, yet each one's tactics varied enormously.

"Jim" likes to ride the wind. At 38 years of age, he figures that he and most of his clients can afford to absorb the risks associated with stock market speculation. He puts 20 percent of his assets in a cash reserve and uses the remaining 80 percent to day trade in the NASDAQ market, investing heavily in technology-oriented companies. As a result, Jim has earned an incredible 300 percent return in the past three years.

"Bruce" has taken the opposite approach. Concerned over the hugely inflated Dow, he has removed his investors' money from the stock market and placed it in a Swiss bank account, where he is earning a meager 2 to 3 percent. My mother would have loved the security Bruce's "bunker" mentality offers. Most of his clients, though, are none too thrilled with his strategy. If the market crashes, Bruce will be an overnight hero. If not, he may find himself without clients.

"Henry" prefers to mix and match. He takes 50 percent of his clients' assets and puts the money into bonds, CDs, cash accounts, and Treasury bills. He uses the other 50 percent to buy into high quality companies through the stock market. It's not a very exciting strategy, but Henry has garnered a 15 to 16 percent return for his investors, which is more than anyone familiar with the history of investing could hope to gain.

And "Kevin" is a market timer. He uses a sophisticated computer program to predict market swings, and he buys and sells accordingly. Thanks, at least in part, to our decade-long bull market, this strategy has paid off well for his clients. Kevin has beaten the odds more often than not, and he has earned about 30 percent per year.

Which of the four advisors would you feel most comfortable working with? My friend Matt, who gleefully tells of putting "everything he has" into Internet stocks this year, would undoubtedly love Jim's style. Matt admits that he has a very high tolerance for risk and, so far, his gambles have paid off.

My mother, on the other hand, would not have been able to sleep at night if she knew that Jim had any measure of control over her money. Like so many older people for whom security is of supreme importance, she would, as I noted, much prefer the slow and steady pace of Bruce's strategy.

Most of us, I believe, would gravitate toward middle-of-the-road counselors like Henry or Kevin. Even though market timing has gotten a lot of bad press, especially within Christian circles, it is not necessarily an unwise strategy (and we'll talk more about investment strategies in the coming chapter).

Personality Matters

In addition to the risk tolerance factor, you want a financial advisor whose personality complements your own. I know where my own strengths and weaknesses lie, and I have chosen a financial advisor who fills in the gaps. "George" is a deep thinker, an introspective man who is not prone to take risks. I, on the other hand, tend to take risks with my own money that I would never recommend to anyone else. George is a good balance to these urges, but I can't help testing him from time to time, just to keep him on his toes.

"George," I said one day not long ago, "I want you to take a couple of thousand and buy this stock." I named one of the more volatile stocks I could think of at the time.

He pulled some information from his computer and I could hear the doubt in his voice. "That stock is pretty unstable, Larry."

"Maybe so, but I think it looks pretty good," I said. We went back and forth for a few minutes until I finally convinced him to buy it—not only for me but for his own portfolio as well.

Before I hung up I said, "George, you and I both know I am not going to buy that junk. I don't buy junk. Why did you let me talk you into that?" "Because you are so persuasive," he said.

"But that's exactly why I use you as my financial planner!" I laughed. "You're supposed to offset my persuasive tendencies. I can talk myself into some high-risk investment; you need to be strong enough to tell me when it is a bad idea."

One way to determine how well you and a particular counselor will complement each other is to give him or her a copy of the personality test included in the previous chapter and then compare your results. If your graphs are identical, chances are that you will each make the same investment mistakes. On the other hand, if the results conflict too much, you and your advisor will have a hard time agreeing on anything.

If you are a "high S-C" (the supporter pattern) and your advisor is a "high D" (the dominant type), you may find yourself being intimidated and pressured into financial decisions you might otherwise not make. Review the evaluation material included in the last chapter, and choose a planner whose strengths, weaknesses, and overall personality provide a good balance to your own.

Other Traits to Consider

One of the first choices you will have to make as you look for a financial counselor is whether to work with a fee-only planner (who gets paid either a flat fee or a percentage of the assets he or she manages for you) or a product salesperson (who earns a commission on any financial products, such as life insurance or mutual funds, that he or she sells as part of a financial plan).

Fee-only financial advisors may be your best bet if you're looking for objective, unbiased counsel. Since they don't make any money from the products or investments they recommend, fee-only advisors don't tend to push any one particular product. And because they typically deal with sizable investments, they often have a broad range of knowledge about many different types of investments and investment vehicles. Plus, because of their investment buying power, these advisors may have access to certain funds or managers that you might not be able to access on your own.

But therein lies a drawback to the fee-only approach. Because the fees can run as high as $500 per hour or 1 to 2 percent of the assets you're investing, this type of counsel is often best suited to investors who have at least $500,000 to invest—people who actually *need* the advisor's far-reaching expertise and who are fully prepared to pay the high fees that professionals demand.

Middle-income investors may prefer to work with product salespeople, typically those whose financial advice takes a much smaller bite out of their investment dollar. These advisors make their money from the products they sell; you don't pay for the advice, only for the actual products or investments you choose to purchase as part of your overall financial strategy.

The key is to be sure that the product the advisor is selling is one that you actually need. If you only need life insurance, for example, you may find that an insurance agent can give you both investment advice and insurance products at a fraction of what you would pay a fee-only counselor for the same counsel.

No matter which type of financial advisor you choose, start your interview process by looking at the advisor's track record.

Has he or she worked with clients whose needs and goals were similar to your own? What sort of a return has the advisor been able to earn for these clients? (If it is less than 5 percent per year over any five-year period, you'd be better off taking a do-it-yourself approach. Even Treasury bills or CDs can return 5 percent.) Ask if it is possible for you to obtain an anonymous copy of a financial plan that the advisor has done for another client whose situation is similar to yours. That way, you'll know what sort of information you can expect to get for your money.

While you're at it, check the advisor's credentials. Avoid amateurs and newcomers. I personally would not recommend any financial planner who has been in the business for less than a decade. You want someone who has seen a couple of downturns and who knows how to keep a level head in a volatile investment climate. Everybody has to learn the ropes sometime, but it will be better for you if your advisor has cut his or her teeth with somebody else's money.

Another factor to consider is the advisor's overall financial knowledge. Just because someone has a CFP (Certified Financial Planner) designation after his or her name does not necessarily mean that person can apply the information. If I were looking for a top-notch advisor, I would test prospects by asking questions about a product with which I was very familiar. If the advisor appeared to know at least as much as I did about the subject, I would figure that he or she had a good depth of knowledge in other areas as well.

Likewise, if you are interviewing a financial counselor who claims to be a Christian, don't shrink from asking specific questions about his or her views on handling money. The Bible has some very clear instructions about issues like debt, saving, investing, and giving; and, as a Christian, you want to be sure that your advisor both understands and applies these principles to his or her own life.

Finally, choose a financial advisor that you and your spouse both trust and feel comfortable working with. Husbands, don't assume that your wives don't care about financial matters or that they won't understand them. Women are very astute and, in many cases, they actually handle the family finances.

And again, since a woman has better than an 80 percent chance of outliving her husband, it is absolutely critical that she participates in and approves of the financial decision making.

Make Your Own Choices

Choosing a qualified financial advisor is only one step on your road to effective investing. Ultimately, you are the one who must make the choices about how and where to invest. Your advisors will give you counsel and direction, but they should not be expected to make your decisions for you. After all, nobody cares more about what happens to your money than you do.

I am always amazed when people I have never met send me checks—sometimes for large sums of money—with instructions to "just invest this for me." Of course, I've never done it; I simply return the checks. How could I intelligently invest money (even if I were an investment counselor, which I am not) for people I don't know the first thing about? Don't ever give such broad license to any financial advisor. Not only is it poor stewardship of your God-given resources, but you could lose a lot of money in the process.

As with so many other financial issues, the Bible does not offer a specific formula for choosing an investment advisor or for deciding how much confidence to place in your advisor's counsel. Rather, the Lord gives us a broad channel within which we can operate. *"The way of a fool is right in his own eyes, but a wise man is he who listens to counsel"* (Proverbs 12:15). *"Without consultation, plans are frustrated, but with many counselors they succeed"* (Proverbs 15:22). These verses speak to the value of seeking wise counsel as you make your investment decisions. So exercising wisdom is the "bare minimum" God asks of us as we develop a financial strategy.

On the other end of the spectrum is the inescapable fact that it is God who is in control. As the Bible says, *"The mind of man plans his way, but the Lord directs his steps"* (Proverbs 16:9).

My primary objective in this book is to show you how to invest effectively for the year 2000 and beyond. Your financial goals, your investor temperament, and your ability to seek wise counsel are all-important pieces of the overall puzzle. The bottom line, though, is not how carefully you establish and pursue your goals, how discriminating you are in selecting a financial advisor, or even how talented you are at picking the winners in the stock market. What really matters and what will, ultimately, dictate your long-term effectiveness as an investor is where you place your trust.

If your hope for the future is in your stockbroker or some other financial advisor, it is misplaced. Instead, your confidence must be in God alone. Remember, *"He who gives attention to the word shall find good, and blessed is he who trusts in the Lord"* (Proverbs 16:20).

Sooner or later (and again, my guess is that it will be sooner), the robust economy that Americans have come to take almost for granted will begin to unravel. But, as Christians, that should not affect the strength or placement of our trust. No matter what the economy does, we can face the future with confidence—a deep confidence in God's character and His sovereignty. Our trust is in Jesus Christ, the One who *"is the same yesterday and today, yes and forever"* (Hebrews 13:8).

And I don't know of any financial advisors, even those who are tops in their profession, who can make that claim. Choose an advisor who accepts God as his or her primary source of wisdom also.

"How blessed is the man who does not walk in the counsel of the wicked, nor stand in the path of sinners, nor sit in the seat of scoffers! (Psalm 1:1).

12

Principle Five:
Choose Your Strategy

Mark was one of my closest friends. He died a while ago, but I have vivid memories of the times we spent together and of how he could always make me laugh, especially when he recounted his investment misadventures. Some of them are classics.

For instance, one time he talked two of his buddies (both doctors, like him) into buying shares in a registered stud quarter horse. Mark had it on good authority that the horse was a record holder in the racing world and that the stud fees investors could expect to earn would be phenomenal.

The horse was a record holder; at least that much was true. But when Mark and his friends finally got to see their investment, they learned the rest of the story. The horse was a gelding. (It could not reproduce!) "I'm a doctor!" Mark exclaimed, when he filled me in on what had happened. "Buying a gelded stud horse is about the worst mistake a licensed physician could ever make! Whatever you do, don't tell my wife!"

The stud-horse fiasco was probably the centerpiece in a

fairly miserable investment career suffered by Mark and his friends. Medically, they were tops in their respective fields, but when it came to investment strategies they inevitably found themselves following bad advice.

Like so many investors, they tended to wait until everyone they knew was buying a particular stock or mutual fund before they "stepped up to the plate." By then, the upward trend would have run its course, and almost as soon as they bought it the stock price would cycle down again.

Ever hopeful for a recovery, the threesome would wait as their stocks continued to fall and their advisor said to "hang on." Finally, though, their optimism would fade. Figuring that they'd better bail out before their investment was totally worthless, they would decide to sell, usually at the rock-bottom market price. Sometimes the cycle would recover and start all over again and the stock (or whatever) would cycle up. More often than not, though, once they invested, it was the kiss of death to that investment.

Market cycles are inevitable, which is, in essence, what makes trying to time the market so enticing to some investors. In this chapter we'll look at the pros and cons of this strategy, as well as at the alternative: buying an investment and holding it for the longer term. Both of these strategies have upsides, as well as downsides; the tactic you ultimately choose depends on many factors, including the following.

- What you believe will happen to the economy in the days and months ahead.
- Your age and your income needs.
- Your investor temperament.

You want an investment strategy that fits your temperament and your needs. Remember, if you can't sleep at night you probably have the wrong strategy. *"Anxiety in the heart of a man weighs it down, but a good word makes it glad"* (Proverbs 12:25).

Market Timing: Buying Low and Selling High

Market timing is, in a nutshell, an investment strategy aimed at avoiding market downturns. Market timers try to decide when the market has peaked, to sell their assets at the maximum value, which obviously is rarely possible. Then, when they perceive the market is in its deepest trough, they buy in again. Market timing is very difficult, and often the most sophisticated timing program will miss the trends. More often than not the average investor will wind up like Mark and his colleagues, buying in at or near market peaks and selling during an investors' run.

As a general rule, when everyone around you (from your neighbors to your newspaper) is hyping a particular stock, or the market in general, you can be fairly certain that it is closing in on its high point. Beware of buying any investment that has been in the media spotlight for very long.

Professional market timers rely on extensive mathematical and computer-generated models to help them predict market trends and get in and out at the right times. Jerry Wagner, president of Flexible Plan Investments Ltd., sees market timing as an investor's natural response to the stock market cycles. In an article entitled "Why Market Timing Works," he maintains that there are "a growing number of timers who consistently outperform the market over a full market cycle, both bull and bear markets." Furthermore, Wagner notes, "When risk-adjusted return is used as the standard measure of performance . . . even the average market timer outperforms the market by a notable margin."[1]

Even though nobody can predict market peaks and valleys with 100 percent accuracy, Wagner cites numbers that he believes give market timers a statistical advantage over investors who take the buy-and-hold approach. He points to the three phases of a market cycle: a correction or downturn, then a recovery to the breakeven point, and finally a move to new highs.

And he notes that in the years since the Dow Jones Industrials recorded its first value in 1885, the market has spent 32 percent of its time in the correction/downturn phase, 44 percent in the recovery phase, and 24 percent in the growth (or bull market) territory. For the buy-and-hold investor (who makes money when the market is above the breakeven point), these numbers translate into less opportunity to make money than to lose it. As the following graph indicates, in a typical market cycle a buy-and-hold investor will be productive only 38 percent of the time, meaning that the investor is in a "down mode" for nearly two-thirds of the cycle.[2]

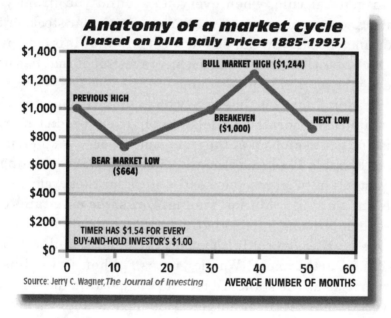

Wagner admits that market timers do not have to have a perfect track record when it comes to knowing when to get in and out of the market. Rather, he says, merely avoiding *a significant portion* of a decline, and not the entire drop, gives a timer extra leverage and more dollars. Looking at the amount of money that a market timer (who sold at the top) would have had when the market bottomed out, versus the amount that his buy-and-hold colleague would have had at the same time, Wagner traces the more-than-100-year history of the Dow Jones. He concludes that for every $1 the buy-and-hold person has, the market timer will have anywhere from $1.26 to $1.54.[3]

Wagner also asserts that from 1985 to 1990 (a time frame that includes the 1987 bear market) market timers incurred a significantly lower level of risk (some 40 to 60 percent less) than investors who followed the S&P 500.[4]

So why isn't everyone jumping on the market-timing bandwagon? For one thing, just because a mathematical model theoretically works when applied to historical markets does not mean that it will perform that well in reality. Furthermore, many investors recognize that past history is no guarantee of future performance and, as Wagner admits, few investors can ever time a single market cycle to perfection, much less repeat the feat from year to year.

Indeed. In his excellent book, *Winning the Loser's Game*, Charles Ellis calls market timing a "wicked" idea, ripe with seductive possibilities. As Ellis tells us, $1 invested in the S&P 500 from January 1960 to June 1990 would have compounded to $19.45. But, Ellis continues, "If the same $1 had been taken out of the market for the best 10 months of those three decades (for just 3 percent of the whole 30-year period) the value at the end of that period would only have been $6.58."[5]

On the flip side, if you could have avoided the 10 worst months, your $1 would have climbed to $63.39.[6] It's tempting, isn't it? But who's to say which 10 months you might wind up missing?

Another drawback to market timing is that unless your assets are held in retirement accounts and can be shifted in and out of funds within those accounts, a sell-off can result in capital-gains taxes. Piled on top of that are the commissions you'll have to pay on your transactions, as well as the losses you will incur when you guess wrong about which way the market will go, which undoubtedly will happen from time to time.

All that being said, I believe that the sustained duration of today's bull market, as well as its record-high stock prices, puts market timing in a very favorable light—at least as a short-term strategy. As I noted earlier, with price-earnings ratios at astronomical and unprecedented levels, we are overdue for a major market correction. And avoiding the big losses is the heart and soul of market timing.

As a case in point, let's look at America Online, the current blue chip for Internet stocks and the only Internet firm listed among the ranks of the S&P 500. America Online has a market value (total stock value) of nearly $200 billion (as of this date), putting it at or near the top of our country's 10 best companies in terms of market value. A look at AOL's real value, however, tells a different story: In a 1998 comparison of U.S. companies, the Internet giant ranked 311th in profits, 415th in sales, and below the 500 mark in tangible assets.[7]

In April of 1999, AOL had a price-earnings ratio (PER) of about 700. If that number were magically shaved down to 30 (or eight points higher than the stock market average in 1929 when it collapsed), AOL would still have to generate net profits of about $6.7 billion per year to justify its $200 billion market value.

Only one American company, General Electric, was able to make that much money in 1998. America Online, in other words, is grossly overvalued by traditional standards. If you were to buy and hold it now, my guess is that you would lose over the next five years. (Of course, that's just an opinion, and it's only worth what you pay for it, which in this case is whatever you paid for this book.)

The Buy-and-Hold Approach

The buy-and-hold approach is exactly what it sounds like. You buy shares in a stock mutual fund or other property, with the intention of holding on to them for the long term. Often, the purchases are made through a strategy known as "dollar cost averaging." The idea behind dollar cost averaging is that you buy stocks on a regular basis, regardless of their price on any given day (that is to say, you buy them when they're high and also buy them when they're low). Then, when all the purchases are averaged out, overall you will have paid a nominal median rate for the stocks.

All you need to do is (1) invest the same amount of money each time you buy, and (2) purchase stocks at regular time intervals (usually monthly). How much you invest and how often you do it is entirely up to you. The important thing is to stick with your plan.

In theory, dollar cost averaging works because having a constant dollar investment allows you to buy more shares when the price is low and forces you to buy fewer shares when it is high. In other words, you buy more at "bargain" prices and less at higher prices.

Even though a sustained bull market can cut into profits for dollar cost averagers, the strategy has significant advantages for investors who are trying to take the emotion out of investing. (In a bull market, you would obviously show greater gains if you invested a lump sum of money early on instead of stretching your buying opportunities over a period of time.) With the simple formula that drives dollar cost averaging, you don't have to make monthly investment decisions or judgment calls; it is all automatic.

If you don't have the temperament (or the nerves) to stay the course during a market downturn, dollar cost averaging can help protect you from knee-jerk reactions or a tendency to follow the crowd. (Remember, as my doctor friends learned all too well, following the crowd is not a position you want to assume when it comes to strategic investing.)

In other words, it all goes back to your temperament, your

age, and your investment goals. The investment strategy you choose depends on whether you can ride out market downturns without having your nervous system wrecked by anxiety, and it depends on whether you have time to wait for the market to recover.

Investing If You're Over 60

I recommend that older investors learn to live on a budget before settling on an investment strategy. It helps to know how much it costs to live, both currently and in the future, and to clearly determine where that money will come from. Perhaps some of your income will come from Social Security, some from a retirement account or pension plan, and some from veteran's benefits. When you add all your sources of income, the difference between that amount and what you will need to live on is the amount of money you will need to earn from your investments.

For instance, suppose you need an additional $10,000 per year on top of what you expect to receive from Social Security, your pension plan, and other benefits or income sources. And let's say you have $500,000 in nonreplaceable funds, such as cash from the sale of your home, personal savings, or a severance bonus (to name a few). My recommendation would be to take $200,000 of that money and invest it in something with reliable fixed earnings over a long period of time: good-quality corporate bonds, certificates of deposit, Treasury bills, tax certificates, or rental property from which you can earn an income. The key to securing at least $10,000 a year in investment income is to invest the $200,000; this is easily doable in the current economy.

Once you have your fixed income secured, consider having some amount of at-risk money that you can risk in the market. Personally, as I noted earlier, I have adopted the 30/70 policy, investing 30 percent of my assets in stocks that tend to fluctuate with the overall market. I put the remaining 70 percent in investments over which I have some measure of control: residential rental properties, CDs, annuities, and other relatively low-risk, low-return "safe havens." I know that in an up market these investments won't make as much money as the other 30 percent of my portfolio, but they will be very stable and secure in a down market.

Once you have settled on a fixed-income amount and an amount that you are willing to take some risks with, your third step is to find a good, professional financial planner. We've already covered how to seek wise counsel: Pick someone who (1) has an excellent track record, (2) shares your investment philosophy and understands your temperament, and (3) can work with the strategy you have chosen.

If the planner can earn more money for you (after commissions) than you can earn on your own by investing in quality stocks, bonds, and mutual funds, then you probably have made a wise choice. If not, go find someone who can.

And, incidentally, I encourage you to do your giving as you earn your money. If you have already tithed on the money that you put into your retirement account or your investment portfolio, don't forget to tithe off any increase that you earn. Don't stop giving simply because you're getting closer to retirement or because you no longer have a salary. God's principles for giving apply to retirees as well as to those who are still in the workforce.

Questions and Answers About Retirement

For older investors, choosing an investment strategy often goes hand in hand with retirement planning. The decisions you make about *when* to retire, and even *why* you want to retire, will directly impact your future income needs.

When should you retire? People often ask me whether it is better to retire at age 62 or age 65, from a Social Security standpoint. If you retire when you are 62 years old and begin drawing on your Social Security plan, you will get less money than you will if you wait until you are 65. Even so, *the typical 65-year-old retiree would require at least eight years of earnings at the higher rate in order to recover what would have been earned between ages 62 to 65.* In other words, from a strictly economic standpoint, you'd be better off retiring at age 62 than at age 65.

Putting financial issues aside for the moment, you must also ask yourself whether you want to retire earlier or later. Let's say you are 60 years old and your company offers you an early retirement buyout. Do you have peace about leaving your job? Do you sense God calling you to stay or to leave? If you don't like your job, you may find it easy to walk away. But if you like what you're doing and you find personal fulfillment in working, you need to weigh the psychological consequences of leaving against the benefits you'll reap from an early retirement package.

If your plan is to trade in your briefcase for a set of golf clubs or a new set of luggage and to spend the bulk of your time on the links or traveling, or some other leisure-oriented activity, you might be better off staying at work. Statistically speaking, the probability of a 65-year-old retiree reaching his or her 75th birthday is only about half that of a 65-year-old man or woman who continues to work during those same 10 years.[8]

If, on the other hand, your goal is to leave your job and embark on another vocation (paid or volunteer) or some missions-oriented work, you might find yourself more fulfilled than ever before. And the financial rewards of an early buyout package could help make your post-retirement dreams a reality. But don't wait until after you retire to figure out how you want to spend your time; consider your options before you find yourself out of a job with nothing to do.

From an economic standpoint, you also have to weigh your lost earnings against the money that your company will give you if you take early retirement. Suppose you are making $50,000 per year and, to entice you to retire at age 60 instead of age 65, the company offers you a lump sum of $250,000 above and beyond all other benefits. The money is the same whether you earn it over a five-year period or receive it all at once, but your *potential for increasing the money through investing is greater if you take the lump sum up front.* In this case, early retirement makes sense financially.

But let's say your salary is $100,000 and the buyout plan is still $250,000. Under this scenario, you will forfeit half the money you could have earned if you had stayed in your job another five years. That may not be such a good deal.

Another decision you may need to make is whether to take your settlement all at once or through a lifetime annuity. Suppose you can choose to receive $250,000 in a lump-sum payment or get $28,000 per year for as long as you live. If you can take the $250,000 and earn at least $28,000 a year (11.2 percent) for the rest of your life through investing, take the lump-sum settlement. If you can't, then choose the annuity. (If you do, though, make sure that the annuity is payable to your spouse if something happens to you.)

Why do you want to retire? Many of us have a tendency to put so much emphasis on the financial results of retiring that we forget the bigger issue: Why do we want to retire? And is it what God wants us to do?

From a biblical perspective, the only reference to retirement is found in Numbers 8:24–25, where the priest is instructed to retire from his temple duties at age 50. Any other reference is indirect, such as the Proverbs 6:6–8 passage in which the ant stores up provisions in the summertime for the lean winter months. We know that, in general, as we get older, our income ability declines; so it only makes sense to stockpile some of our earnings in anticipation of that time. But I believe the concept of abandoning useful work altogether, other than for health reasons, is not biblical. It is not good stewardship of time, talents, or treasures.

The exception to this statement is found, of course, in the person who retires because he or she believes God is leading him or her to something else. In this case, if you have funds set aside, so that you can follow God's call without being dependent on your former salary, quitting your job makes perfect sense. But, again, don't wait until the prospect of retirement stares you in the face to do your planning; think and pray beforehand about what God might want you to do down the road.

Investment Advice for the Under-60 Crowd

If you are under age 60, your investment strategy should be planned around your temperament. Do you have a buy-and-hold mentality, or are you a market timer at heart? If you can ride out market downturns without worrying about the future, try dollar cost averaging.

If your bent is toward market timing, my recommendation is that you hire a financial advisor who is an expert in this area. I am not recommending any particular individuals; rather, I suggest that before you hire anyone you check him or her out for yourself.

Personally, I always utilize some form of market timing. If you truly believe that a market downturn is coming, it only makes sense to pull your assets out, even if the downturn does not ultimately occur. In that case, all you will have missed is some of the gain. Missing a significant loss is much more important to me.

Furthermore, the probability of an economic downturn triggered by Y2K (or other economic factors like those we've already discussed) makes *now* a good time to avoid a potential downturn. If you decide to do this, I recommend parking the assets in something very safe: bank CDs, Treasury bills, or money market accounts with a large, reputable brokerage firm.

Personally, I'm going to sit on the sidelines for the first half of the year 2000. If Y2K turns out to be a nonevent and the market continues its logic-defying climb, all I will have missed is six months' worth of gains, and I will reenter the market later in the year. But if the market does head into a spiral as a result of Y2K (or the simple fact of the long-overdue correction), I will have missed some major losses. That's just my opinion. Take it for what it's worth.

Looking Beyond Y2K

Having told you that I think market timing makes sense in our current financial climate, let me back up and offer a big-picture perspective on investing. Over the long run, most investors do not have enough assets to hire a professional market-timing service and, if they opt to try market timing on their own, they will probably lose a lot of money. Over the long term, buy-and-hold is generally a superior strategy. With that in mind, I want to wrap up this chapter with a few investment pointers for you to keep in mind.

1. Develop a long-term perspective. *"A good man leaves an inheritance to his children's children, and the wealth of the sinner is stored up for the righteous"* (Proverbs 13:22). Look back over the past 50 years. If you had bought and held on to quality companies like General Motors, Chrysler, Ford, General Electric, Xerox, IBM, and others, you would have done quite well. Hundreds of millions of dollars have been made by buy-and-hold investors who chose these companies early on. And don't let today's volatile market scare you off. Remember, God is not surprised by anything that happens, and He is still in control.

2. Everything that goes around comes around. One of the very first lessons I learned in economics school is that market cycles are inevitable. Don't be deceived by a long upward trend; the market will eventually come back down and level itself out. If you learn to expect market swings, they will not have the power to fill you with foolish exuberance or unwarranted fear.

3. Buy quality, not popularity. It doesn't matter whether you are choosing stocks, property, or friendships; quality is more important than popularity. Don't follow the hottest fads; rather, choose stocks (and friends) you can count on for years to come.

4. Count the costs. Buying and selling costs will be higher for more frequent trading. As you hone your investment strategy, don't forget to factor in the fees you will have to pay when you buy or sell stocks, as well as any capital-gains taxes you will incur.

5. Don't "dig up your carrots." If you are investing with a long-term perspective, don't check on your investments every day and second-guess your decisions. If you've done your homework and evaluated the companies properly, just leave your "carrots" where they are and trust that they will grow with time. I have a computer program I use to check stock prices, and I purposely do not put my long-term stock buys into the program, to avoid the temptation to "dig up my carrots" to see if they are growing.

6. Learn to see time as a resource. You don't need a lot of money to make a lot of money; you just need a small amount of money and a lot of time. Not long ago, I read a story about a cleaning woman who, as a single mother, put her two children through college and graduate school and then left $500,000 to the university where she worked so the school could set up a scholarship endowment for underprivileged children.

The woman had never earned more than $15,000 per year, but she always saved and invested 10 percent of her paycheck. She didn't use an investment advisor; rather, she simply bought stock in the companies that made the products she used and liked— everything from soap to automobiles. As you take stock of your assets, remember that time can be your greatest resource.

Once you have defined your overall investment strategy, you can begin to choose the specific investments that will shape your portfolio. Just as your time horizon can make a significant difference in the long-term success of your strategy, so can the investments themselves.

In Chapter 14 we'll explore several different types of investment vehicles you can use to diversify your assets. And in today's market, diversification could spell the difference between financial stability and wild fluctuations.

———

1. Jerry Wagner, "Why Market Timing Works," *Journal of Investing*, Volume 6, Number 2, Summer 1997.
2. Ibid. (graph).
3. Ibid.
4. Ibid.
5. Charles Ellis, *Winning the Loser's Game* (New York: McGraw-Hill, 1998).
6. Ibid.
7. Jeremy J. Siegel, "Are Internet Stocks Overvalued? Are They Ever," *Wall Street Journal*, April 15, 1999.
8. *Social Security Administration 1989 Annual Report.*

Principle Six:
Investment Values and Moral Values

I have a good friend who runs an investment company that manages hundreds of millions of dollars of other people's money. My friend's firm invests in a lot of companies. And, like most good investment advisors, he does his homework. He checks out a company's financial statements, looks at their goals, and considers their overall health within their particular industry.

But my friend doesn't stop there. Before he makes any investment, he (or one of his professional team members) visits the company's headquarters. He interviews the directors, including the president, to discover everything possible about the people who will lead the company 20 or 30 years down the road. He asks to see written goals and scrutinizes the company's five- and 10-year plans. As he puts it, "You can't tell if a company is sound just by looking at the building or analyzing its profits. Anybody can buy an impressive-looking building, and with the kind of market we've had in the past few years even an idiot can turn a profit."

What my friend looks for, overall, is quality. Not short-term, flash-in-the-pan kind of appeal, but the strength, vision, and inherent value that will allow a company to prosper and grow for more than one generation. Picking quality companies is, for my friend, a personal responsibility. Because of the large amounts of money that his firm can funnel into various companies, he can create a market, to some degree. When word gets out that his company has endorsed a particular company, its stock value usually goes up.

Over the years, my friend has picked some major winners. He bought Microsoft and America Online in their infancy, before the rest of the investment world recognized their potential. He bought Chrysler and General Motors after they had bottomed out, confident that they had "the right stuff" to stage a major comeback. And, during the past five years, he has been combing through Internet stocks to find the companies that will endure long after the technology they represent has become commonplace. And make no mistake, today's high-flying Internet stocks may be risky investments, but the technology itself is here to stay; and it will reshape the way we do just about everything, from buying groceries and sending mail to teaching children and transacting business.

So how does my friend spot the winners? In today's market, buying quality can be tough. Most new things can look good at first—whether stocks, clothes, cars, or people. But on closer inspection, these things are not always the best. The flashiest clothes don't always last the longest, the shiniest car is not necessarily the most dependable, and the tallest and most handsome man doesn't always make the best leader. Consider, for instance, two famous kings from the Bible.

Saul was Israel's first king: *"a choice and handsome man, . . . from his shoulders and up he was taller than any of the people"* (1 Samuel 9:2). Saul looked like he'd be a terrific king. In fact, the Israelites crowned him with a great celebration; yet, it wasn't long before he began making some serious mistakes. Eventually, his true colors became apparent: He was an evil, arrogant, and often insane man and, ultimately, God rejected him.

By contrast, David, who succeeded Saul as king, did not have much in his favor. The youngest of eight brothers, he worked in the most humble of jobs: a shepherd for his father's flock. When David went out to meet Goliath in the now-famous confrontation, the giant looked him over and, seeing that David was only a boy, he despised him. *"Am I a dog,"* Goliath sneered, *"that you come to me with sticks?"* (1 Samuel 17:43).

Obviously, there was nothing regal or imposing about David's appearance. He didn't look like much of a king; yet he was the one God chose to lead his people. *"The Lord has sought out for Himself a man after His own heart, and the Lord has appointed him as ruler over His people"* (1 Samuel 13:14). *"God sees not as man sees, for man looks at the outward appearance, but the Lord looks at the heart"* (1 Samuel 16:7).

When it comes to investing, spotting the difference between the Sauls and the Davids is sometimes difficult. I believe that there are two basic factors to consider before making any long-term investment, either in individual stocks or mutual funds. First, you need to assess the quality of the investment itself. And, for Christians, you need take a careful look, from an ethical standpoint, at where you put God's money. In other words, you need to consider an investment's *values,* as well as its *value.* First, we'll look at value.

Buying Quality

The Bible says, *"Do you see a man skilled in his work? He will stand before kings; he will not stand before obscure men"* (Proverbs 22:29). If Warren Buffett (financier mentioned in Chapter 7) had been asked to translate that particular passage, his version might have been, "Quality always pays off in the long run."

To identify quality in any investment, keep three principles in mind.

1. Look for companies that are reasonably priced. By "reasonably priced," I mean the price of the stock(s) is not disproportionate to traditional norms (the norm is what a prudent buyer will pay in the current market). When I shop for a car and see the prices, I have to remind myself, this is not 1964, when you could buy a new car for $2,600. Now the "bargains" are found by saving $3,000 on a $20,000 car.

Appearances can be deceiving, and I'm just as guilty as the next person of falling prey to the temptation of bargain hunting. Recently, when I was helping my grandson choose some clothes, I spied a golf shirt (for me) on sale for $19.95. I've already confessed my love for golf, and I have paid a lot more for a good quality golf shirt in the past.

Thinking I was getting a great deal, I bought the $19.95 shirt. The first time I put it in the dryer, however, it shrunk to my grandson's size, so now it belongs to him. In retrospect, the more expensive shirts usually are a better value; they last a lot longer. Whether you are buying golf shirts or mutual funds, the moral of the story is, The lowest-priced item is not necessarily the least expensive.

2. Look for companies that will return a fair share of their profits. This bit of advice is always sound, but the specter of Y2K and an economic downturn makes it all the more timely. Here's what I mean.

Over the years, my personal portfolio has included such quality stocks as Coca-Cola, General Electric, General Motors, Westinghouse, Sears and Roebuck, Wal-Mart, Microsoft, and Dell Computers. I bought these stocks because I knew that if they even did their basic business they would make money and, therefore, would pay dividends. And, if their stock price rose in value, that was an added bonus, but it was not all I was anticipating when I purchased the stock.

If you buy company stocks with an eye toward earnings (rather than just appreciation in their stock prices), you don't have to worry about market timing. And, you won't need to check on these stocks, at least not on a daily or weekly basis. And even if Y2K takes the market down for awhile, these are the companies that will survive and recover. Of course, no investment is risk free; however, if you are looking for quality, go with companies where earnings are more important than price.

3. Invest in companies that will be around for a long time. Like my friend from the investment firm, look at where the company wants to be in five or 10 years and how it plans to get there. As an individual investor, you may not be able to personally interview the company's leaders or tour their facilities, but you can access their financial statements. If a company or mutual fund offers stock for sale, it must by law provide a prospectus. In addition, you can access historical financial data via the Internet. I use *www.compuserve.com* or *www.hotbot.com* to access this information. In lieu of that, good mutual funds will do the investigating for you.

Value counts in emerging technologies as well. As I noted earlier, if you had been able to invest in quality companies in the early days of electricity, radio, and television, you would have done quite well financially. Many companies did not survive the revolutionary changes those technologies brought, but those that were able to keep pace and even lead the pack emerged stronger than ever. Likewise, there are a handful of well-managed, reasonably priced companies dotting the ranks of today's Internet offerings. If you can identify and buy into one of these survivors, you likely will reap some significant financial rewards.

Of course, very few novice investors can spot these solid investments; it's like looking for a needle in a haystack of investment hype. As I recommended earlier, you probably would be better off putting your money into a growth mutual fund, and in the hands of a professional money manager, instead of trying to do all of the research and tracking on your own.

Remember, before you buy into any mutual fund, check out its ranking and its track record through the resources I previously mentioned: *Consumer Reports*, *Money* magazine, *Forbes*, the *MorningStar* report, and the monthly *Sound Mind Investing* newsletter. *(Sound Mind Investing* is published by a Christian friend, Austin Pryor, and can be found on the Internet at *www.soundmindinvesting.com.)*

That said, let's look at index funds (which Warren Buffett, incidentally, recommends as an investment option for his followers). An index fund is a special type of mutual fund whose sole objective is to mirror the performance of a market index.

You can buy into an index fund through any one of a number of fund organizations: Vanguard, Fidelity, T. Rowe Price, and Scudder. Here's how they work. The fund organization—let's say, for example, the Vanguard Group—sets up a mutual fund that is made up of the very same stocks that the market indexes use to determine their value.

You can invest in a Dow Jones index, a NASDAQ index, a Standard and Poor's index, or any number of other index funds. In each of these cases, the portfolio manager will invest in the same securities (quality stocks) that are used in calculating the index. The fund will make or lose money to the same extent that the overall index does.

Suppose, for example, you invested in the Standard & Poor's 500 stock index.

If the S&P 500 gained 16 percent in any given year, your index fund would grow by that same 16 percent, less fees. For average or novice investors, few investment options offer more in the way of simplicity and returns—better than the majority of professional investors earn by trying to pick the winners.[1]

Of course, index funds do have their downsides. Because they stay fully invested at all times, index funds offer no protection during market downturns or periods of weakness. If a bearish market takes stocks down by 30 percent, index funds in general will fall similarly. For this reason, if you like the "autopilot" approach of investing through index funds, be sure to diversify your portfolio with other types of investments.

Be Careful Where You Invest God's Money

Buying quality is a financial objective, but buying ethically acceptable investments is a biblical objective. God's Word says, *"The integrity of the upright will guide them, but the falseness of the treacherous will destroy them. . . . The perverse in heart are an abomination to the Lord, but the blameless in their walk are His delight"* (Proverbs 11:3, 20).

Several years ago, a clothing company, headquartered in San Francisco, took a public stand against the Boy Scouts of America, a Christian organization, because the Scouts would not allow homosexuals to serve as troop leaders. It was reported that company executives went to the local United Way organization and used its corporate muscle to get the Boy Scouts removed from the United Way's list of beneficiaries.

I thought that this company's actions were both unwise and unfair, and I wrote to them to ask that they and the United Way reverse their policy. I received a curt letter in reply, the gist of which was that I should "mind my own business" and that the company's policy was "equal rights for homosexuals" (regardless of the Boy Scouts' rights).

The issue, as I saw it, was not about equal rights. It was about a powerful company trying to force its belief system onto an organization whose very mandate runs counter to those beliefs. Since my letter had had no effect, I took a look at the mutual funds in my portfolio. Several of them did include that company's stock; and, in fact, the stock had done quite well. Even so, I directed my financial planner to sell my shares in any mutual funds that had even a minority interest in the company.

Next, I went on my radio program and recommended that our

listeners do the same thing. Tens of thousands of people apparently took my advice, sold their stock and, in some cases, even went so far as to mail their jeans back to the company.

Not surprisingly, the company threatened to sue me. I encouraged them do so, thinking that such a lawsuit would be terrific publicity for my position: namely, that this manufacturer was not pro-family. The lawsuit never materialized. (Interestingly enough, though, the company has since fallen on hard times and, over the past few years, the value of its stock has plummeted.)

When I began my personal crusade, the company represented a good value, financially speaking. But value and, for that matter, quality aren't everything. Look at this verse. *"The perverse in heart are an abomination to the Lord, but the blameless in their walk are His delight"* (Proverbs 11:20). Which camp would you rather be in?

Money—specifically, your money—is merely an outside indicator of an inward spiritual condition. *Where* you put your money speaks volumes about what you believe. Then how can we as Christians invest with a clear conscience before the Lord?

It's not easy. For starters, you don't always know where a mutual fund manager will invest your money at any given time, no more than you know whether your bank has made a loan with "your" money to a crooked businessman or an anti-Christian organization. You simply cannot check every transaction to ensure that your money is working on behalf of kingdom principles—unless, of course, you are willing to stash all your cash under your mattress and monitor every last dollar.

You can, however, invest intelligently. Although there are undoubtedly many more ways to filter your options, here are three tactics many investors use to decide how and where to put their money.

1. Invest in "socially conscious" or "socially responsible" funds. These mutual funds have "screens" designed to weed out companies that engage in activities or practices investors find objectionable. But even though socially responsible investing is attracting an ever-larger following (mostly, as you might imagine, among liberal activists who want to impact the way business and society operate), some Christian investment advisors do not wholeheartedly embrace this strategy.

One reason is that many socially conscious funds have traditionally turned in only mediocre performances. Just because a company's philosophy lines up with your value system does not make it a sound investment; if an investment is not going to make money, there is really no point in pursuing it. For Christians who want to make their voices heard in the corporate world, the advisors argue that there are more effective ways (such as product boycotts) to get a company's attention.

Socially responsible investing is difficult but not impossible. There are conscientious companies developing good programs to screen for blatantly immoral companies. One that I use regularly can be found on the Internet at *www.crosswalk.com*. As Christians living in a fallen world, we cannot avoid all financial contact with secular businesses or organizations, but we can, and should, do the best we can.

2. Vote with your money. Even though I generally encourage Christians to avoid investing in companies with questionable moral policies, there are exceptions to every rule. For instance, I regularly give money to my local public television station, even though I disagree with the philosophy behind much of their programming, particularly as it pertains to topics like abortion (which they paint in a favorable light) and evolution (which they tend to treat as fact, rather than theory).

Because of my regular giving, I have become what this station considers a "major donor." Now when I write to them with a complaint or suggestion about their programming, I get an immediate response, often with an apology enclosed. As with nonprofit organizations, when they get negative letters from major donors, it catches their attention and prompts them to take remedial action.

Likewise, I have personally given money and time to political candidates whose positions on certain pro-family issues were, at best, questionable. My hope, in these cases, was to impact their thinking. So far, this strategy has been reasonably effective. I have seen a number of politicians take pro-family stands, and vote accordingly, as a result of our Christian support.

Voting with your money can work just as well on Wall Street. Over the years, I have invested small amounts of money in organizations that appeared to be operating contrary to God's Word, in the hope of influencing the company from within. I like to show up at stockholders' meetings (or at least vote by proxy) so that my voice will be heard. If, after two or three years there has been no change in the company's direction, I sell whatever holdings I have and focus my energies elsewhere.

3. Support the good guys. In today's market, there are many publicly held companies that, although not being overtly Christian, are very pro-family and pro-Christian in their policies. Britain's Cable & Wireless Company, a large international long-distance telephone service provider, is a case in point.

Cable & Wireless has chosen not to advertise or endorse companies whose products or policies run counter to family values. I use their excellent local and long-distance services, and I encourage others to do the same.

Keep your eyes and ears open. When you see or hear about a company that is willing to take a stand for the values you hold dear, check to see if the report is true. Then, consider taking a similar stand by using its services or by buying its stock in a show of financial support.

Remember, as God's people we are not here just to make money. Our goal should be to honor the Lord with our wealth. As the Lord said, *"For what is a man profited if he gains the whole world, and loses or forfeits himself?"* (Luke 9:25). There is nothing inherently wrong with gaining wealth; and if you buy quality, the value of your portfolio will likely increase. Just don't lose your values, your faith, or your relationship with God in the process.

---

1. Austin Pryor, *Sound Mind Investing* (Chicago: Moody Press, 1996), 157.

14

Principle Seven:
Diversify Your Assets

Claire and Allen had been out of college for only a year when they got their first telephone call from a stockbroker. Peter had been a fraternity brother of Allen's at the college, and he said he was working to build a client base. "Do you and Claire want to buy any shares in a regional meatpacking company that is poised to corner the market?" he asked.

Never having purchased any stocks before, and with only about $1,000 in their savings account, Allen and Claire were hesitant to part with any of their hard-earned money. Finally, though, they decided to buy $500 worth of the stock.

Less than a month later, their investment had doubled in value. When Peter called with another buying opportunity, this time in a trucking company, the couple didn't hesitate. They sold the meatpacking stock, pocketed their $500 gain, and used the money to buy into the trucking company, fully expecting the market to repeat its magic on their behalf. Bit by bit, though, the trucking company's stock value eroded. Allen and Claire held on for a grueling six months, ever hopeful for a rebound, until their $500 investment in the trucking company had entirely vanished.

"Well, we made $500 and lost $500," Allen said. "I guess we're even."

"Yes," Claire agreed, "but let's not invest in anything else. I don't think I can stand the stress."

During Allen and Claire's short-lived venture into the investing world, they broke virtually all of the commonsense rules in the book: used an unproven financial advisor, adopted a short-term mentality, speculated with money they could not afford to lose, and put all of their eggs in one basket. All in all, they were fortunate to exit the market with their meager savings still intact!

Diversification (putting your financial "eggs" in several different baskets) is the backbone of any sound financial strategy. The Bible points to the wisdom behind this principle: *"Divide your portion to seven, or even to eight, for you do not know what misfortune may occur on the earth"* (Ecclesiastes 11:2).

The theory behind diversification is that different assets or types of investments respond differently to fluctuations in the overall economy. By allocating your resources to several different market sectors, you can lower your overall risk and better stabilize your asset base. Diversification goes beyond just buying different companies' stocks. Good diversification includes a variety of industries (auto, computer, banking), as well as totally diverse areas of the economy (rental property, land, tax certificates, bonds, and so on). This will help to offset rises and falls in diverse areas of the economy.

The uncertainty that marks today's financial climate makes diversification all the more important. Risk-tolerant investors who have built their portfolios strictly around Internet and technology stocks, for example, could see their gains disappear in an incredibly short period of time. On the flip side, ultraconservatives who have kept their money in cash or U.S. government securities may not incur the risk of loss; yet, they have opened themselves up to the very real threat that over a period of time their holdings will not keep pace with inflation and living expenses.

I realize the official inflation rate looks very low today. Remember, however, the overall inflation rate is a composite figure and may not represent your true inflation rate. For example, if you don't buy a new home, the inflation in new homes is irrelevant. But if a sizable percentage of your income is consumed by real estate taxes, school costs, and new cars, your inflation rate is considerably higher than the official rate. Diversification must take into account more than just inflation. Risk of loss (stock value) is lessened by diversification also.

How you choose to diversify your assets depends on factors like your age, financial goals, and personal risk tolerance. In this chapter we will look at a number of widely recognized investment options and consider the strengths and weaknesses of each. Even though no portfolio is 100 percent "recessionproof," through diversification you can strengthen your financial position as you prepare for the new millennium.

Stocks and Mutual Funds

If you want to invest in the stock market and don't feel comfortable making your own decisions, look for a good-quality mutual fund. Mutual funds run the gamut from the most conservative to the most speculative and offer several advantages over individual stock purchases. For one thing, you get built-in diversification, because mutual funds invest in a variety of different stocks. For another, mutual funds are run by professional fund managers, which gives you a level of expertise that you may not have on your own, unless you can afford an experienced financial planner.

To find a mutual fund that suits your investor temperament and financial goals, you can access most rating services on the

Internet. Or you can go to your public library and access the resources noted in the Appendix.

Look for funds that parallel your investment strategy. For instance, if you are investing for a long-term goal (such as retirement), look at growth mutual funds. One possibility is to put the bulk of your assets in one or more of these funds that is neither ultraconservative nor overly speculative and leave it there for several years.

Bear in mind that any fund can do well for a year or two, so look for funds that perform well over a longer period of time. I personally look for funds that have appeared in the top 10 listing for at least 10 years.

When shopping for mutual funds, another factor to consider is whether you want to purchase no-load or loaded funds. You can't get something for nothing, and mutual funds are no exception. With a no-load fund, you don't pay an up-front commission; rather, the sales charge is averaged into the fund's annual fees. With a loaded fund, you pay the commission when you buy into the fund.

The conventional wisdom among many financial planners is that, over any seven-year period of time, it really doesn't matter whether you buy loaded or non-loaded funds; all other funds being equal, the costs will average out about the same. I tend to prefer no-load funds because of the freedom they give me to buy and sell without paying a commission each time I make a transaction. However, if you need professional help, you must pay for it; hence, the loaded fund.

Although I believe that mutual fund investing still represents the greatest potential for the average investor, a word of caution should be noted. As I've commented repeatedly in this book, I expect the next couple of years to bring some significant changes to our current market, and a 20 percent drop in the value of stocks would not be improbable. Thirty-eight percent of Y2K experts expect a 20 percent loss in stocks (with a recovery in

2001). Forty-five percent expect unemployment in the U.S. to reach 6 percent in the year 2000, as a direct result of Y2K.[1] With this in mind, you need to consider diversification when making investment decisions.

For 30- to 35-year olds, who should be investing in equity markets, mutual funds (including those in 401[k] or other retirement accounts) represent a solid investment option. If you fall into this age group, go for growth rather than speculation as you choose your funds.

For 40- to 50-year olds, equity investing should be balanced with other types of investments. Even so, I believe that the market still has tremendous potential, particularly with quality companies, and the Internet looks like the engine to drive the economy for at least the next 10 years.

For investors who are older than 60, only a portion of their assets should be invested in the equity markets. Again, the majority of this money should be in high-quality bonds, or bond funds, or at least in blue-chip stocks in a variety of industries.

Bonds and Bond Funds

This investment area is another one in which buying quality is important. Unlike stocks, bonds are an obligation (a debt) on the part of the organization that issues them. Treasury bills, for example, are debts of the U.S. government. Municipal bonds are debts of a city, county, or state. Corporate bonds are debts of the companies that issue them. In each of these cases, if you buy a bond, the issuer has to pay the agreed-upon interest at the specified times or lose its credit rating.

Because of their stability and the fixed rate of income they offer, bonds are a good investment choice for people who are 60 or older. If you buy a $10,000 bond that pays 7.5 percent interest per year for 10 years, and you plan to hold it for a 10-year period, there is no risk (except company failure). The bond issuer is obligated to pay you the interest owed and then, after 10 years, they must redeem the bond, meaning that you get your $10,000 back.

Some investors, however, buy and sell bonds as a speculative commodity, just as they do stocks. Let's say you bought that same 10-year bond for $10,000 at 7.5 percent interest and then interest rates in the 10-year bond market dropped to 6 percent. At that point, your bond would become worth more than you paid for it. Another buyer might purchase it from you for $11,000, so he or she could get a higher-than-market rate of interest.

By the same token, if interest rates rise, your bond would be worth less than what you paid for it—that is, if you wanted to sell it. (Remember, if you are planning to buy and hold a bond, rather than trying to sell it, there is no risk involved, except the stability of the issuing agency.)

Real Estate

A third way to diversify your portfolio is through real estate. Virtually everyone is involved in real estate, either as a homeowner, landlord, or tenant, which makes real estate one of the few investments in America that almost everyone understands.

Real estate represents diversification as an investment for two reasons. First, it represents a long-term capital asset. If you own a home, you do not have to pay taxes on the gains as it appreciates in value. And if you live in the home at least two years, the new tax laws exclude up to $250,000 (per individual) or $500,000 (per couple) in capital gains. Up to those limits, there are no taxes on the property's appreciated value. And you can repeat this process every two years! Tax-wise, it's one of the best investment deals. Just remember, though, most women don't look at their homes as *investments*. They look at them as *purchases*.

Another reason real estate is appealing is that it's an investment that you can actually use. Personally, I plan to live in my home for a few more years and then sell it and scale down. Thus, unlike stocks or bonds, it has daily utility to me.

Rental properties also help to achieve portfolio diversification. As an investment, rental properties can provide a hedge against the volatility often seen in stocks, bonds, and other intangible assets. The downside to rental properties, though, is that if you own them you automatically become a landlord, which means that you are responsible for repairs, painting, plumbing, and other maintenance work. You could, of course, hire a property manager to do these things for you, but that may not be feasible, from an economic standpoint.

If you choose to invest in real estate, either by buying your own residence or buying rental properties, remember the three important principles: location, location, location. The more undeveloped or untested a property is, the more it will expose you to the risks associated with speculation. If you want more information on investing in real estate (advice from how to screen prospective tenants to figuring out whether to sell or rent your home) my book, *Investing for the Future* (Chariot/Victor, 1992), covers this topic in greater detail.

Precious Metals

"Is it a good idea to buy gold?" is one of the most common questions I hear these days, especially from people who are concerned about a stock market slide or the potential for inflation in the future.

At one time, silver was a hot commodity, but when the silver market collapsed in the early 1980s, it fell out of favor with investors and, as an investment, it has been depressed ever since. To a lesser degree, the same can be said of gold.

Many wealthy investors buy gold as a means of stabilizing the value of their money. In an inflationary period, when currencies are devalued, gold tends to increase in value (although not always).

Today, though, inflation is virtually nonexistent, making the need for gold less of a priority than it has been in the past.

Even so, it would seem prudent to invest some portion of your assets (5 percent or less) in a precious metal like gold. If inflation takes off again, and we see a return to the runaway prices of the 1970s, shift a higher percentage of your assets into gold. If not, and the value of gold continues to drop as it has in the past decade, don't panic. One of the rules for effective investing is *don't look back*. When you make a carefully considered investment decision, don't second-guess yourself at every turn.

Gold has been purchased as a hedge against currency fluctuations for thousands of years. People can't make it, and governments can't counterfeit it. Over the long run, gold will recover its value. But, it's been my observation that when average investors speculate in gold or silver, they usually lose.

Some time ago, one of my business partners bought $10,000 worth of gold. Almost as soon as he bought it, the price started to plummet and within a week it had dropped by 25 percent. "Should I sell?" he wanted to know.

"Probably not," I answered. "You bought it for the long haul. Don't dig up your 'potatoes' to see how they're doing."

A couple of weeks ago, he cheerfully informed me that his gold was down nearly 40 percent! I told him to inform me the next time he invested in something so I could warn others.

Tax Certificates

Another investment option, and one that is not commonly discussed, is tax certificates, which can be purchased from municipal, county, or city government. Tax certificates are created when individuals fail to pay the real estate or ad valorem taxes on their property. The municipality typically notifies the property owner and then, if the taxes remain unpaid for several months, the tax collector's office will issue a tax certificate or lien equal to the amount that is due and put it up for sale.

Diversify Your Assets

Tax certificates are sold at public auction. The buyer pays the taxes that are due. The property owner then becomes responsible for paying the amount that is owed in taxes, plus an assigned interest charge (usually from 12 to 18 percent). Every tax certificate I have bought has always been redeemed, along with the interest due.

But it doesn't always happen that way. If the property owner does not redeem the certificate, and you have to keep paying the taxes, after three years the property belongs to you. This can be a low-cost way to pick up a piece of property for the equivalent of three years' tax bills.

Remember the risk and return factor, because there is potential risk. I have a friend who bought a tax certificate on a piece of property when real estate values were at a low point. The property owner never redeemed the certificate so, after three years, ownership transferred to my friend. At that point, the municipality tripled the taxes and, as a result, my friend owed several thousand dollars per year on a piece of property he never really wanted in the first place!

Furthermore, he found out that an old oil dump contaminated the property, and the EPA ordered him to clean it up, at a cost of several hundred thousand dollars! Fortunately for my friend, he found a nonprofit group that could use the property and the EPA agreed to waive their restrictions based on how the property would be used by that organization.

The moral of the story? There is risk in *everything*, and when you are talking about a high rate of return, like you can get with a tax certificate, there is a correspondingly higher rate of risk.

Collectibles

There are all sorts of ways to diversify your assets; I've briefly covered some of the more well-known investment vehicles. One final option I want to mention is collectibles: stamps, coins, antiques, gemstones, and other rarities. Even though collecting can provide a significant amount of personal satisfaction to investors who enjoy "the hunt," collectibles, by and large, are a very risky investment.

For one thing, you have to have a certain level of personal expertise to evaluate the items before risking your money. And assigning a specific dollar value to any given item, or an entire collection, is very subjective. For instance, different experts may assign varying values to the same piece of jewelry or the same antique, making it difficult to evaluate the true value. And during a recession, assets like stamps, numismatic coins, or other rarities that have a very limited market are sometimes illiquid (hard to sell). In short, my advice is to collect anything that you like; but do it because you enjoy the collection and not because you expect to profit from it, unless you're willing to spend the time and effort to become an expert yourself.

For many years, I restored antique automobiles. Through trial and error I learned which cars appreciated the most and concentrated only on those. But mostly I collected the cars because I enjoyed them. My family and I had many good times in the cars and, ultimately, I had a fair rate of return (if I disregard my personal labor). Collecting can be fun, but it requires a high degree of specialized knowledge.

Looking Down the Road: Diversify Yourself

For most investors, diversification is strictly a financial term, applied only to an investment portfolio. But as you look toward the new millennium, and particularly if you are approaching retirement, consider the advantages of expanding your options by diversifying your own skills, training, and talents.

A good friend of mine retired from a successful medical practice several years ago. After he retired, he went back to school—this time to a trade school to learn how to be a plumber. He doesn't work full time, but by doing odd jobs he truly enjoys one or two days a week he has been able to supplement his income by

$300 to $500 per week. He also has made his hobby/trade a ministry by helping widows and single moms without charge. They get a lot of fun out of telling their friends that their handyman is an M.D.

Another friend is a retired airline pilot who traded in his wings for a paintbrush and easel. A lifelong art lover, he began painting landscapes as a hobby long before he retired. When he discovered a thriving market for his talent, he launched his own business and is now a much sought-after artist.

Do you have a skill or talent that could be marketed? If a backup career seems elusive at first, keep your eyes open to the opportunities the Lord may provide. I know of one former executive who parlayed a fascination with woodworking into an incredibly lucrative business, in which he salvages decrepit old wooden structures and transforms them into unique picture frames.

As you weigh your diversification options, work with your financial advisor to ensure that your portfolio reflects a healthy mix of investment options. But don't stop there. As the Bible says, *"You do not know what misfortune may occur on the earth"* (Ecclesiastes 11:2). Recession or not, the new millennium is sure to be marked by change. As we move into the year 2000 and beyond, the better equipped you are to adapt to changing times, the better off you will be.

---

1. M.J. Zuckerman, "45% of Y2K experts worried," *USA Today*, June 10, 1999.

15

Bonus Principle:
Avoid Investment Debt

Take a look at this," Rick said, sliding a black notebook across the mahogany surface of his desk. "I think you'll be pleased with what we've done."

Julie and Doug leaned forward to study the pages. Rick was right: the notebook *was* impressive. All of Julie and Doug's financial statements, income tax records, and investments were neatly categorized. Brightly colored tabs identified their various goals: college education, insurance, retirement, estate planning, and giving. There was even a current cash-flow analysis and a series of five-, 10-, and 20-year projections for the future.

"It looks great," Doug agreed. "Can we talk through some of the numbers?"

"Of course," Rick agreed. As a financial advisor, showing his clients how to understand and apply a comprehensive financial plan was one of the things he liked best about his job. Positioning the notebook so that all three of them could see the pages, he slowly explained each aspect of the financial plan.

Twenty minutes later, Julie spoke up. "I don't mean to get

ahead of you," she said, "but I don't see where paying off our mortgage figures into the plan."

"It's right here," Rick said, flipping through a few pages. "You've got a 30-year mortgage, and you've been in your house for three years. So far, your payments are pretty much going toward the interest, but . . ." (Rick ran his finger down the column of numbers) "you can see how your equity builds as time goes by."

"I thought we were going to try to pay off the loan early," Julie said, glancing at Doug. "At least, that's what we talked about, and that's what our pastor is advising Christians to do."

Rick shifted in his chair and shot a glance at Doug. It was impossible to read Doug's thoughts. "Well," Rick said, clearing his throat. "Let me see if I can explain this to you.

"It doesn't make very good sense, from a financial perspective, to pay off your mortgage early. Number one, you would lose the tax deduction you're currently getting for your home." Rick turned to the tax planning section of the notebook and showed Julie and Doug how the mortgage deduction factored into their taxes.

"And number two," he continued, "if you take the money you would put toward paying off your mortgage early and invest it in the stock market, you can earn a whole lot more than what you would save in interest by paying off your house.

"Let me show you what I mean." Rick rummaged through his files and pulled out a graph like the one on the next page.

"Let's say you had $100 to invest each month. If you put it into your house, here's how the money would grow." Rick traced his finger along the equity line. "And here," he continued, pointing to the higher stock market line, "is what would happen to that same $100 if you put it into the market at an average earnings of 12 percent."

Julie looked at Doug again. "I understand what he's saying," she said, "but I thought we agreed that paying off our home was a top priority." "We did," Doug conceded. "Rick, I agree with what you've shown us here, but that goal remains unchanged. We're just not comfortable with debt, and the sooner we can get rid of that mortgage, the better."

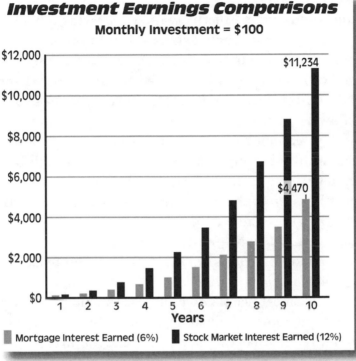

Investment Earnings Comparisons
Monthly Investment = $100

Mortgage Interest Earned (6%)   *Stock Market Interest Earned (12%)*

"Well, that's your call, of course," Rick said stiffly. "I'll run some numbers on paying down your mortgage and see where that puts you. For now, though, let's look at some of your insurance needs."

Later, sitting alone in the quiet of his office, Rick reflected on Julie and Doug's desire to be debt free. *Some people*, he concluded disgustedly, *just don't get it.*

Mortgage Versus Market

On the face of things, most investors don't see themselves as borrowing in order to invest. And very few financial planners would counsel their clients to use credit cards or take out a bank loan to invest in the stock market (although that's not altogether unheard-of). But credit cards and bank loans aren't the only ways to borrow money.

As Julie and Doug instinctively knew, carrying a home mortgage in order to funnel their extra cash into the stock market was, in effect, using debt to finance their investments. And, as a financial counselor who has advised countless people on this particular subject, I can tell you that Rick's logic has some significant flaws.

In theory I cannot argue that Julie and Doug would make more money through the stock market than through building equity in their home (unless, of course, they put their assets into the market just *before* the downturn). As we learned earlier, 38 percent of the time, the amount of money being earned in the stock market is apt to be greater than the amount of interest being paid on most of today's home mortgages. But to look at that statistic alone is to ignore the bigger picture.

For starters, most people *don't* invest the money they would have used to pay down their mortgage. Instead, they spend it, with the net result that the money is gone, no investment has been made, and the mortgage still remains.

Another factor to consider is that, according to the Social Security Administration, the majority of 65-year-old retirees still carry a mortgage on their homes; and, on average, these senior citizens have 20 years to go before the debt is paid off! I don't mean to burst anyone's bubble, but I have to say that it's fairly optimistic for a 65-year-old to think he or she will live another 20 years in the first place. Furthermore, having a mortgage when you no longer earn a salary is not a good plan.

Still another problem with the money-in-the-market-not-the-mortgage logic is that there is always the possibility that you will lose some or all of the money you invest. But, regardless of how the market performs, your mortgage is not going to disappear. If your stock market holdings take a dive, your mortgage lender won't care. He will still expect you to make the payments.

Finally, you have to consider your peace of mind, which, in my opinion, is more important than any amount of money and therefore a higher priority than the size of your investment returns. Over the years, I have personally talked with hundreds, perhaps thousands, of Christian families who have made the commitment to pay off their homes. I have yet to meet anyone who, having met this goal, has looked back with regret. Instead, virtually all of the testimonies I hear focus on God's goodness and the peace that these people enjoy as a result of owning their own homes.

Again, I am not debating the fact that stock market investing, at least in recent years, has been far more lucrative than home ownership. But before you listen to the conventional wisdom, prayerfully consider all of the factors. Paying down debt is a sure thing. Investing is always conditional.

Other Ways to Borrow to Invest

As I told you in an earlier chapter, one of the most alarming trends I have witnessed on our radio program is the number of people who are over their heads in credit card debt, even as they commit money to their 401(k)s and other retirement accounts. For all intents and purposes, what these families are doing is using their credit cards to invest in the stock market.

Two factors make this practice a bad idea. First, the interest rate owed on credit cards (generally anywhere from 16 to 21 percent) is almost guaranteed to exceed the average earnings in the stock market. And what's more, when the market drops, the credit card debts will not be forgiven. Profit or loss, the credit card usury still has to be paid.

Another too-common practice is for people to borrow money from their 401(k) accounts or their IRAs. Instead of using credit cards or traditional loans to pay for cars, homes, or college education costs, many families simply take money out of their retirement accounts, agreeing to pay it back by a certain time. There is nothing inherently wrong with this practice, and it is certainly more satisfying to pay yourself interest on a loan than to pay it to a bank or credit card company; however, borrowing from your 401(k) can have some very negative consequences.

For one thing, retirement accounts often are used as a vehicle for stock market investing. When you take money out of the account, you incur an opportunity cost: The gains you would have realized if you had left your money in the market are gone. You have lost the opportunity to make the potential gains you otherwise would have earned.

A more significant problem is the risk that you might not be able to repay the money on time. If you miss the deadline, the amount you borrowed is treated as a "premature withdrawal," meaning that you have to pay a penalty of 10 percent of the outstanding balance, as well as the federal and state income taxes on the withdrawal. The outstanding balance is added to your annual income that year. That can be an unwelcome burden and a serious setback to your long-term plans.

The Surety Factor

Let me reemphasize that there is nothing wrong with investing in the stock market. As I've said more than once, I believe the stock market represents the underlying value of our economy in general. But borrowing to do so does not make good common sense.

Furthermore, borrowing for investment purposes (in general) violates the biblical principle called surety. *"He who is surety for a stranger will surely suffer for it, but he who hates going surety is safe"* (Proverbs 11:15). Surety, in its simplest form, is taking on an obligation to pay without having a guaranteed way to pay it back.

For instance, let's say that you spot what looks like a terrific investment deal on a piece of land that costs $10,000 and the owner offers to finance it for you. You put $1,000 down and sign a note that obligates you to pay the landowner the remaining $9,000. Under the terms of your note, you agree that if you fail to make the payments on the loan, the landowner will have the right to reclaim the land *and* keep all the money you have already paid. Not only that, but your note also has a deficiency agreement, so that if the land sells for less than the amount that you still owe on the note, the landowner has the right to sue *you* for the difference.

Sound harsh? It is, but it's also the way business is often done these days. For instance, if you can't meet your mortgage payments, the mortgage lender can foreclose and resell your house. If your loan contract has a deficiency agreement, the lender then can sue you for any deficiency. (Some states protect home buyers from deficiencies on first mortgages.) That is *surety:* The borrower guarantees to pay the balance regardless of the collateral. This rule applies to all surety loans, including credit cards and personal loans.

The one certain way to avoid surety (and the only scriptural way to borrow money) is to use an *exculpatory note.* In layman's terms, an exculpatory is a statement that says, if you cannot repay a loan, the lender gets to keep whatever money you have paid thus far, along with the collateral (land, car, stocks pledged against the loan), but there is no deficiency clause. In other words, you have a sure and certain way to repay the debt; surrender the collateral.

Twenty-five years ago, non-surety notes were commonplace. Fifteen years ago, they were becoming rare, and today they are virtually nonexistent. Today, when someone borrows, that person is in surety—a practice that violates the biblical principle of borrowing.

Our Get-Rich-Quick Culture

With all of the drawbacks that accompany debt, you may ask, "Then why do so many people borrow money to invest?" Likewise,

"Why have millions of Americans embraced speculative investing as a cornerstone of their financial strategies?"

I believe the answer to these questions lies in our collective desire to become wealthy, without a lot of work—in other words, get rich quick. It all goes back to the mindset we covered earlier: "Why work so hard when easy money can be made in the stock market?" and "Why should we wait to save money for the things we want when it is so easy to borrow?"

God's Word says, *"A faithful man will abound with blessings, but he who makes haste to be rich will not go unpunished"* (Proverbs 28:20). Similarly, *"He who tills his land will have plenty of bread, but he who pursues vain things lacks sense"* (Proverbs 12:11).

If you take at least one principle away from this book, I pray that it will be to avoid the get-rich-quick mentality. To that end, there are three basic rules to remember.

1. Don't risk money that you cannot afford to lose. I cannot tell you how many families I have counseled who have risked money they needed to live on (especially borrowed money) and lost it all. Although my heart goes out to these people, the verse that always comes to mind in such situations is, *"A man with an evil eye hastens after wealth, and does not know that want will come upon him"* (Proverbs 28:22). Investing—even speculative investing—is fine if you clearly assess the risk and if you have the surplus money on hand. Doing it with money that you can't afford to lose is foolish.

2. Don't get involved in any venture or investment that is too complicated to understand. Remember my friend on the golf course—the one I talked into buying into the Internet? He didn't know anything about the Internet, other than what I had told him, which wasn't much, and yet he was ready to jump on board with a significant sum of money that could not be replaced. That attitude of leaping before you look is typical of the get-rich-quick mentality. But, *"By wisdom a house is built, and* *by understanding it is established; and by knowledge the rooms are filled with all precious and pleasant riches"* (Proverbs 24:3–4).

By and large, most people make money doing what they do best in their businesses and careers. By contrast, the vast majority of ordinary people who lose investment money do so by risking it in something they really don't understand. In today's investing world, where speculative day traders exaggerate their profits and downplay their losses, the temptation to leap before you look is greater than ever before. But a word to the wise: No matter how much money your friends *say* they are making in the stock market, don't always believe it; and, if you don't fully understand what they are doing, stick with your plans.

Does that mean you cannot invest in a mutual fund unless you understand its inner workings? No, that's the fund manager's job. But you have to have some degree of knowledge and expertise before you risk your hard-earned money in any investment. Again, you need to get educated. Reading is the best and cheapest way to start.

3. Don't make quick decisions. Day traders (stock market investors who buy and sell on an hourly basis) may be the epitome of get-rich-quick investing. Granted, some of them have made money in recent years, but it will be interesting to see what happens in the years to come. *"The plans of the diligent lead surely to advantage, but everyone who is hasty comes surely to poverty"* (Proverbs 21:5).

On this last point, let me tell you how I make financial decisions, from a timing standpoint. On any decision that involves more than a $1,000 commitment, I wait three weeks. If it is less than $1,000, I wait three days. Granted, I have missed a few "golden opportunities" by waiting; but for every good deal I have missed, I have also avoided about a thousand bad ones.

Remember the pyramid schemes I discussed earlier? Typically, pyramid investments violate all three of these rules. The salespeople emphasize borrowing to get involved (on the theory that, if you borrow to invest, you will be more motivated to work hard to get that money back). They want you to get involved with something that you really cannot understand. (I defy anyone to look at a pyramid-marketing scheme and explain, coherently, how it is supposed to operate!) And finally, they want you to make a quick decision, even going as far as to challenge you not to leave the room after a sales presentation until you have made a commitment to "make yourself rich."

Whether you are contemplating a pyramid scheme or an investment in stocks, bonds, mutual funds, or real estate, there are three rules that always make sense: *Don't risk what you can't lose; if you don't understand it, don't do it; and don't make hasty decisions.* And, the older you are the more important it becomes to follow these guidelines.

You can go broke investing. It's been done before, and it will be done again and again. If you are more than 60 years old, you should not take excessive risks with your money. As your career winds down and your income ability begins to level out, you may find it increasingly difficult to replace any money you lose when an investment sours. Don't let anyone (your planner or your brother-in-law) pressure you into investing in something you don't fully understand or that you have not had adequate time to consider and pray about. Even if you are a senior citizen, you have plenty of time to put your money to work; don't be in a hurry to get rich, and don't make hasty or ill-considered decisions.

If you are a younger investor, get your priorities in order. Don't max out your retirement fund contributions if it means you have to rely on credit cards to meet your living expenses. Likewise, don't sacrifice your family's shorter-term needs on the altar of retirement. Invest in quality, growth-oriented stocks, but also have a realistic goal to pay off your home, put your children through college, and otherwise reduce or eliminate your debts *before* you shift your investment focus to retirement.

Avoid Investment Debt

I realize that some of the information presented in this book may run counter to the fashionable financial wisdom of today.

- I am encouraging you to pay off your home; others will tell you why you shouldn't.
- I am telling you not to obsess about saving for retirement; society says to save early, often, and all you can.
- I am urging you to take your time about investing; in today's frenetic financial climate, such a carefully considered approach seems (at least in the world's eyes) rather old-fashioned.

But if you follow God's principles of investing, you won't lose—in the long run. If you place a higher value on gaining wisdom than you do on getting rich quick, you can meet any economic scenario with confidence—from a financial setback to a full-blown recession.

Remember that *"wisdom is protection just as money is protection. But the advantage of knowledge is that wisdom preserves the lives of its possessors"* (Ecclesiastes 7:12).

Just because the "economic earthquake" didn't hit the U.S. as it did most of the rest of the industrialized world, that does not mean we are home free. I sincerely trust that the optimists will be correct and that we'll avoid all the negative impact of Y2K and the longest bull market in modern times, *but I don't think so!*

The one certainty I do have is that if we fear God and trust in His ways, we will prosper, even if we lose all of our material possessions. *"Praise the Lord! How blessed is the man who fears the Lord, who greatly delights in His commandments. His descendants will be mighty on earth; the generation of the upright will be blessed. Wealth and riches are in his house, and his righteousness endures forever"* (Psalm 112:1–3).

That says it all.

APPENDIX

Suggested Resources

Books
(Please note that the majority of these books are written by non-Christian professional investors and do not reflect the beliefs of Christian Financial Concepts.)

Bogle, John C. *Bogle on Mutual Funds: New Perspectives for the Intelligent Investor.*
New York, NY: Dell, 1994.

Burkett, Larry. *Investing for the Future.*
Colorado Springs, CO: Chariot Victor, 1992.

Carson, Charles B. *Buying Stocks without a Broker.*
New York, NY: McGraw, 1992.

Downes, John and Goodman, Jordan E. *Dictionary of Finance & Investment Terms, 5th ed.*
Hauppauge, NY: Barron, 1998.

Eisenson, Mark. *Banker's Secret.*
New York, NY: Villard Books, 1990.

Appendix

Linder, Ray. *Making the Most of Your Money: How to Develop a Personal Financial Strategy for Maximum Impact.*
Colorado Springs, CO: Chariot Victor, 1995.

Lynch, Peter. *Learn to Earn: A Beginner's Guide to the Basics of Investing & Business.*
New York, NY: Wiley, 1997.

Lynch, Peter, and Rothchild, John. *One up on Wall Street: How to Use What You Already Know to Make Money in the Market.*
New York, NY: Viking Penguin, 1990.

O'Shaughnessy, James. *How to Retire Rich.*
New York, NY: Broadway BDD, 1998.

Pryor, Austin. *Sound Mind Investing: A Step-by-Step Guide to Financial Stability & Growth.*
Chicago, IL: Moody Press, 1996.

Schwab, Charles. *Charles Schwab's Guide to Financial Independence: Solutions for Busy People.*
New York, NY: Crown Publishing Group, 1998.

Siegel, Jeremy J. *Stocks for the Long Run.*
New York, NY: Business Week Books, 1998.

Spitz, William T. *Get Rich Slowly: Building a Financial Future.*
Old Tappan, NJ: MacMillan, 1996.

Swedroe, Larry. *Only Guide to a Winning Investment Strategy You'll Ever Need: Beyond Index Mutual Funds—The Way Smart Money Invests Today.*
New York, NY: NAL-Dutton, 1998.

Appendix

Magazines and Newsletters

Morningstar Fund Investor
Morningstar Stock Investor
Income Fund Outlook Yield Forecasts
Risk Ratings and Total Return Projections
Sound Mind Investing

Software

Morningstar Principal Plus for Mutual Funds
SnapShot Gold (Christian Financial Concepts)

This list is provided for informational purposes only. The author does not necessarily endorse any advice or counsel given in these resources or by the organizations represented.